Spiritual Classics

Series

World Wisdom
The Library of Perennial Philosophy

The Library of Perennial Philosophy is dedicated to the exposition of the timeless Truth underlying the diverse religions. This Truth, often referred to as the *Sophia Perennis*—or Perennial Wisdom—finds its expression in the revealed Scriptures as well as in the writings of the great sages and the artistic creations of the traditional worlds.

Introduction to Sufi Doctrine appears as one of our selections in the Spiritual Classics series.

The Spiritual Classics Series

This series includes seminal, but often neglected, works of unique spiritual insight from leading religious authors of both the East and West. Ranging from books composed in ancient India to forgotten jewels of our time, these important classics feature new introductions which place them in the perennialist context.

Cover: Koranic inscription from the Friday Mosque,
Shiraz, Iran, 1351

INTRODUCTION TO SUFI DOCTRINE

Titus Burckhardt

Foreword by
William C. Chittick

World Wisdom

Introduction to Sufi Doctrine

Library of Congress Cataloging-in-Publication Data

Burckhardt, Titus.
[Du soufisme. English]
Introduction to Sufi doctrine / Titus Burckhardt ; foreword by William C. Chittick.
p. cm. -- (The spiritual classics series)
Includes bibliographical references (p.) and index.
ISBN 978-1-933316-50-5 (pbk. : alk. paper) 1. Sufism--Doctrines. I. Title.
BP189.3.B8713 2008
297.4'1--dc22

2008002905

Printed on acid-free paper in Canada.

For information address World Wisdom, Inc.
P.O. Box 2682, Bloomington, Indiana 47402-2682

www.worldwisdom.com

To the revered memory

of

Shaykh Muḥammad at-Tādilī

and of

Mulay ʿAlī ben aṭ-Ṭayyib ad-Darqāwī

CONTENTS

FOREWORD TO THE 2008 EDITION

I am delighted to see that World Wisdom Inc. has decided to republish Titus Burckhardt's little classic on Sufism, which first appeared in English in 1959 (translated from the French *Du Soufisme*). The book meant a great deal to me when I first discovered it as an undergraduate forty years ago. I had been studying the Orientalist books on Sufism and after three months had pretty much convinced myself that I knew the topic rather well. This book stopped me in my tracks.

Burckhardt (1908-84) was a prolific author, but few of his writings demonstrate as clearly his intimate knowledge of Sufi theory and praxis. This was his first book-length study of Islamic topics after his initiation into the Darqāwī Sufi order in Morocco in 1934. He was an accomplished and versatile scholar, and his wide-ranging erudition shines through the book. This makes it especially useful for those who are familiar with the Western intellectual tradition or world religions, though it can be disorienting to those already rooted in Islam and unfamiliar with other traditional approaches to wisdom.

Nowadays, the available literature on Sufism is surprisingly diverse, so much so that it is often difficult to see its common denominator. The academic works often have the advantage of an awareness of Sufism's deep roots in the Islamic tradition. The books written by practitioners fill a broad spectrum. On one extreme, some enthusiasts provide no reason to differentiate Sufism from Kabbalah, Christian mysticism, or a New Age concoction. Others claim to present the teachings of traditional Sufi orders, and many do, but sometimes a great deal is lost in translation—by which I mean not only the movement from one language to another, but also the transition from one cultural matrix to another.

Without trying to classify here the various sorts of books on Sufism, let me suggest what sets Burckhardt's study apart. Most forms of Sufism and quasi-Sufism known in the West place a high priority on love. This is well and good, and Burckhardt himself points out that Ibn ʿArabī—the "greatest master" of Sufi theoretical teachings—put love at the pinnacle of concerns. At the same time, however, love needs to be complemented by knowledge and understanding. Those familiar with the great spiritual teachings of mankind are well aware that correct knowledge of doctrine, rites, and ethical prescriptions has always been placed at their foundation. The transformation of the soul that may take place draws its vitality, vigor, and soundness from clear seeing and right understanding. Even a tradition like Zen, which tells us to throw away the books, has produced reams and reams of books telling us why the books are useless.

Within the Islamic tradition Sufism has always been the inspiration for a great variety of literature, all of it deeply rooted in the traditional learning. The shaykhs and spiritual guides knew Qur'ān, Ḥadīth (prophetic sayings), jurisprudence, theology, and often other Islamic sciences as well. They produced popular books addressed to the uneducated and enormously erudite books as well, on such topics as theology, metaphysics, cosmology, spiritual psychology, the stages of spiritual growth, and the inner meaning of the law. They also produced much of the best and most widely beloved poetry of the Islamic languages—Rūmī is far from an isolated example.

Sufism, in other words, was like other branches of Islamic learning in that it was grounded in a tradition of scholarship and study. More than scholars in other fields, however, the Sufis knew that learning was only a tool, not an end. They also knew that with rare exceptions, one could not advance in the path to God without acquiring at least the rudiments of that tool. Of course, God does what He wants and we have nothing to say about it. Moreover, as the Sufi saying has it, "One pull from the side of God is equal to all the good works of jinn and men." Nonetheless, the Sufi shaykhs understood that by and large, God's custom is to pull those who exert effort in following the path of the Prophet and the shaykhs. They remind us that the very urge to learn about God, His prophets, His scriptures, and the path to Him is His pull. The seeking of the seekers is the trace of the pull of the Puller. As the Qur'ān has it, "He loves them, and they love Him" (5:54). The order is not accidental—God's love primes the seekers' pump.

What was so stimulating for me the first time I read Burckhardt was his presentation of Sufism with a seriousness of purpose and a respect for traditional learning that was somehow adequate to the monumental task that Sufis set out for themselves—to achieve the encounter with God already in this life. Burckhardt was far more challenging intellectually than the Orientalist books I had been reading, and also far more satisfying. His major focus is on Ibn ʿArabī, and indeed this book represents one of the first in a Western language by an author not only familiar with Ibn ʿArabī's writings, but also actively involved in attempting to put his teachings into practice. I do not think that I am speaking only for myself when I say that I received my first real taste of Ibn ʿArabī from this book, and it played a significant role in my choice to do a PhD dissertation on his school of thought.

Reading through the book again after a lapse of many years, I should say that Burckhardt sometimes appears a bit too categorical in some of his interpretations of Ibn ʿArabī's teachings. For my own part, it took me twenty years of study before I learned that you can never pin Ibn ʿArabī down. He constantly shifts perspective, especially in his monumental *al-Futūḥāt al-Makkiyya.* What he says in one place may well differ or even disagree with what he says elsewhere. Nonetheless, Burckhardt is right on target in his exposition of the seriousness of the Sufi path and the recognition of the great teachers of the relativity of their own views. In contrast to the theologians and jurists, they tried to dissolve dogmatic knots in the soul. They did everything they could to discourage their disciples from getting stuck in the words and expressions and to urge them to look beyond the words into the invisible reality that is expressed.

In the general Sufi perspective, words have much the same relation to meaning as body has to spirit. The spirit is there at the depths of our souls to be actualized and realized, but this could never happen without our initial embodiment. In the same way, doctrinal expression will be left behind when one achieves the root awareness of the heart, but can never uncover one's own heart without prophetic guidance. This guidance is unpacked precisely in the theory and praxis embodied by the writings and moral character of the great teachers of the past.

Burckhardt stresses the relativity of doctrine with typical precision toward the beginning of Part Three of the book. Like so many other passages, this one lets his intimacy with Sufism shine through. It is a fitting summary of the "Sufi doctrine" he introduces:

> The Divine Reality is at the same time Knowledge and Being. He who seeks to approach that Reality must overcome not only ignorance and lack of consciousness but also the grip which purely theoretical learning and other "unreal" things of the same kind exert over him. It is for this reason that many Sufis, including the most outstanding representatives of gno-

sis such as Muḥyi-d-Dīn ibn ʿArabī and ʿOmar al-Khayyam affirmed the primacy of virtue and concentration over doctrinal learning. It is the truly intellectual who have been the first to recognize the relative nature of all theoretical expressions.

William C. Chittick
Stony Brook University

PREFACE

This book forms an introduction to the study of the doctrines of Sufism. It is, however, necessary first of all to define the point of view from which the subject is approached. The point of view is not that of pure scholarship, whatever may happen to be the scientific interest of the doctrinal summaries which figure in this book; the chief purpose is to contribute to the efforts of those who in the world of today seek to understand the permanent and universal truths of which every sacred doctrine is an expression.

Let it be said at the outset that academic knowledge is only a quite secondary and very indirect aid in assimilating the intellectual content of oriental doctrines—indeed the scientific method which of necessity approaches things from the outside, and thus from their purely historical and contingent aspects, does not set out to promote such an assimilation. There are doctrines which can be understood only from the "inside" through a work of assimilation or penetration that is essentially intellectual[1] and, for that very reason, goes beyond the limitations of discursive thought. Indeed, in so far as it is stamped with mental conventions (not to speak of the agnostic and evolutionist prejudices which determine the outlook of most occidentals), discursive thought even becomes an obstacle. This it is which explains why almost every erudite European who has studied Sufism has mistaken its true position. Men of modern culture are no longer accustomed to think in terms of symbols and so modern investigations are unable to distinguish between what, in two analogous traditional expressions, belongs to the external form and what is the essential element, and for that very reason the erudite European is led to see borrowings by one tradition from another where in fact there is only a coincidence of spiritual vision, and fundamental divergences where it is only a question of differences in perspective or in mode of expression.[2] It is

[1] By "intellect" is here meant, not the reason or discursive thought, but the "organ" of direct knowledge or of certainty, i.e. the pure light of intelligence which goes beyond the limits of reason alone. The theology of the Eastern Orthodox Church, and in particular Maxim the Confessor, calls this "organ" the *Nous*. Sufis would say that the real "seat" of the intellect is the heart (*al-qalb*) and not the brain.

[2] Cf. Frithjof Schuon, *The Transcendent Unity of Religions*, 2nd ed. (New York: Harper and Row, 1975).

inevitable that such confusions should arise since a university training and bookish knowledge are in the West deemed sufficient authority for concerning oneself with things which in the East remain naturally reserved to those who are endowed with spiritual intuition and who devote themselves to the study of these things in virtue of a true affinity under the guidance of those who are the heirs of a living tradition.

In what follows an attempt will be made to show the intellectual perspective of Sufism and to this end its own way of expressing things will be adopted with the addition, where this is possible, of whatever explanations are needed by a European reader. At the same time analogies will be indicated between certain ideas of Sufism and those of other traditional doctrines. To do this does not involve contradicting in any way the point of view inherent in Sufism, for Sufism has always recognized the principle according to which the Divine Revelation, transmitted by the great mediators, takes on different forms corresponding to the different aptitudes of the human groupings called on to receive them.[3] It is well understood that comparisons between different traditions run the risk of being misunderstood; and for the most part Sufi masters have limited themselves to general indications of the universality of the traditions. In this they respected the faith of simple folk, for, if religious faith is a virtuality of knowledge (otherwise it would be merely opinion), its light is none the less enclosed in an emotional realm attached to one particular translation of transcendent Truth. As a result it tends to deny everything that relates to another inspired mode of expression. However, prudence in relation to the faith of a human grouping or collectivity is called for only so long as the sacred civilization which protects that collectivity represents a more or less impenetrable "world". Such a situation may change after an inevitable meeting of two different sacred civilizations such as the meeting of Islam and Hinduism under the Mogul emperors, and all the more does it change when the contours of the great traditional civilizations are breaking down. In the chaos in which we now live certain comparisons are inevitable, at any rate for those who are sensitive to spiritual forms, and it is no longer possible to avoid

[3] This universal law of Revelation is expressed in the Qur'ān, although only by implication: "The Prophet believes what his Lord revealed unto him. The faithful also believe in God and in His angels, His (revealed) books, and His messengers. They say: 'We make no distinction between the messengers of God'" (2:285) and, again: "We have established for every nation rites which it practices" (22:67).

the problems to which such comparisons give rise simply by passing over them in silence.

First of all it is important to understand that, if those whose outlook is esoteric recognize the essential unity of all religions, that does not lead them either to blur the contours of spiritual forms or to overlook the necessity, in its own order, of this or that sacred Law. Quite the reverse is true, for the diversity in the forms of the religions not only shows up the inadequacy of every formal expression in the face of total Truth, but also, indirectly, demonstrates the spiritual originality of each form—its inimitability in which the uniqueness of their common principle is affirmed. The boss of a wheel both unites the spokes and also determines their divergent directions.

This introduction to the doctrine of Sufism is necessarily incomplete. It treats chiefly of metaphysic, which is the basis of everything; method is dealt with only in broad outline, while cosmology receives no more than a passing reference.

In relation to certain aspects of the doctrine here summarized, reference is chiefly made to the "Very Great Master", Muḥyi-d-Dīn ibn ʿArabī (1165-1240 A.D.) whose role in relation to Sufism may he compared to that of Śrī Śaṅkarāchārya in relation to the Vedānta.

Since Sufism is a tradition—that is, the transmission of wisdom divine in origin—there is both a perpetuation in time and a continual renewal by contact with the source which lies outside time. Every traditional doctrine is by definition immutable in essence but its formulation may be renewed within the framework of the given "conceptual style"—and so on the basis of the constants of the tradition—in relation to different possible modes of intuition and according to human circumstances.

PART ONE

THE NATURE OF SUFISM

Chapter 1

AT-TAṢAWWUF

Sufism, *Taṣawwuf*,[1] which is the esoteric or inward (*bāṭin*) aspect of Islam, is to be distinguished from exoteric or "external" (*ẓāhir*) Islam just as direct contemplation of spiritual or divine realities is distinguishable from the fulfilling of the laws which translate them in the individual order in connection with the conditions of a particular phase of humanity. Whereas the ordinary way of believers is directed towards obtaining a state of blessedness after death, a state which may be attained through indirect and, as it were, symbolical participation in Divine Truths by carrying out prescribed works, Sufism contains its end or aim within itself in the sense that it can give access to direct knowledge of the eternal.

This knowledge, being one with its object, delivers from the limited and inevitably changing state of the ego. The spiritual state of *baqā*ʾ, to which Sufi contemplatives aspire (the word signifies pure "subsistence" beyond all form), is the same as the state of *mokṣa* or "deliverance" spoken of in Hindu doctrines, just as the "extinction" (*al-fanā*ʾ) of the individuality which precedes the "subsistence" is analogous to *nirvāṇa*, taken as a negative idea.

For Sufism to permit of such a possibility it must be identified with the very kernel (*al-lubb*) of the traditional form which is its support. It cannot be something super-added to Islam, for it would then be something peripheral in relation to the spiritual means of Islam. On the contrary, it is in fact closer to their superhuman source than is the religious exotericism and it participates actively, though in a wholly

[1] The most usual explanation is that this word means only "to wear wool (*ṣūf*)", the first Sufis having worn, it is said, only garments of pure wool. Now what has never yet been pointed out is that many Jewish and Christian ascetics of these early times covered themselves, in imitation of St. John the Baptist in the desert, only with sheepskins. It may be that this example was also followed by some of the early Sufis. None the less "to wear wool" can only be an external and popular meaning of the term *Taṣawwuf*, which is equivalent, in its numerical symbolism, to *al-Ḥikmat al-ilāhiyyah*, "Divine Wisdom". Al-Bīrunī suggested a derivation of *ṣūfī*, plural of *ṣūfiya*, from the Greek *Sophia*, wisdom, but this is etymologically doubtful because the Greek letter *sigma* normally becomes *sīn* (s) in Arabic and not *ṣād* (ṣ). It may be, however, that there is here an intentional, symbolical assonance.

inward way, in the function of revelation which manifested this traditional form and continues to keep it alive.

This "central" role of Sufism at the heart of the Islamic world may be veiled from those who examine it from outside because esotericism, while it is conscious of the significance of forms, is at the same time in a position of intellectual sovereignty in relation to them and can thus assimilate to itself—at any rate for the exposition of its doctrine—certain ideas or symbols derived from a heritage different from its own traditional background.

It may appear strange that Sufism should on the one hand be the "spirit" or "heart" of Islam (*rūḥ al-islām* or *qalb al-islām*) and on the other hand represent at the same time the outlook which is, in the Islamic world, the most free in relation to the mental framework of that world, though it is important to note that this true and wholly inward freedom must not be confused with any movements of rebellion against the tradition; such movements are not intellectually free in relation to the forms which they deny because they fail to understand them. Now this role of Sufism in the Islamic world[2] is indeed like that of the heart in man, for the heart is the vital center of the organism and also, in its subtle reality, the "seat" of an essence which transcends all individual form.

Because orientalists are anxious to bring everything down to the historical level it could hardly be expected that they would explain this double aspect of Sufism otherwise than as the result of influences coming into Islam from outside and, according to their various preoccupations, they have indeed attributed the origins of Sufism to Persian, Hindu, Neoplatonic, or Christian sources. But these diverse attributions have ended by canceling one another, the more so because there is no adequate reason for doubting the historical authenticity of the spiritual "descent" of the Sufi masters, a descent which can be traced in an unbroken "chain" (*silsilah*) back to the Prophet himself.

The decisive argument in favor of the Muḥammadan origin of Sufism lies, however, in Sufism itself. If Sufic wisdom came from a source outside Islam, those who aspire to that wisdom—which is

[2] This refers to Sufism in itself, not to its initiatic organizations. Human groups may take on more or less contingent functions despite their connection with Sufism; the spiritual elite is hardly to be recognized from outside. Again, it is a well-known fact that many of the most eminent defenders of Islamic orthodoxy, such as ʿAbd al-Qādir Jīlānī, al-Ghazzālī, or the Sultan Ṣalāḥ ad-Dīn (Saladin) were connected with Sufism.

assuredly neither bookish nor purely mental in its nature—could not rely on the symbolism of the Qur'ān for realizing that wisdom ever afresh, whereas in fact everything that forms an integral part of the spiritual method of Sufism is constantly and of necessity drawn out of the Qur'ān and from the teaching of the Prophet.

Orientalists who uphold the thesis of a non-Muslim origin of Sufism generally make much of the fact that in the first centuries of Islam Sufi doctrine does not appear with all the metaphysical developments found in later times. Now in so far as this point is valid for an esoteric tradition—a tradition, that is, which is mainly transmitted by oral instruction—it proves the very contrary of what they try to maintain.

The first Sufis expressed themselves in a language very close to that of the Qur'ān and their concise and synthetic expressions already imply all the essentials of the doctrine. If, at a later stage, the doctrine became more explicit and was further elaborated, this is something perfectly normal to which parallels can be found in every spiritual tradition. Doctrine grows, not so much by the addition of new knowledge, as by the need to refute errors and to reanimate a diminishing power of intuition.

Moreover, since doctrinal truths are susceptible to limitless development and since the Islamic civilization had absorbed certain pre-Islamic inheritances, Sufi masters could, in their oral or written teaching, make use of ideas borrowed from those inheritances provided they were adequate for expressing those truths which had to be made accessible to the intellectually gifted men of their age and which were already implicit in strictly Sufic symbolism in a succinct form.

Such, for example, was the case as regards cosmology, a science derived from the pure metaphysic which alone constitutes the indispensable doctrinal foundation of Sufism. Sufi cosmology was very largely expressed by means of ideas which had already been defined by such ancient masters as Empedocles and Plotinus. Again, those Sufi masters who had had a philosophical training could not ignore the validity of the teachings of Plato, and the Platonism attributed to them is of the same order as the Platonism of the Christian Greek Fathers whose doctrine remains none the less essentially apostolic.

The orthodoxy of Sufism is not only shown in its maintaining of Islamic forms; it is equally expressed in its organic development from the teaching of the Prophet and in particular by its ability to assimilate all forms of spiritual expression which are not in their essence foreign to Islam. This applies, not only to doctrinal forms, but also to ancillary matters connected with art.[3]

Certainly there were contacts between early Sufis and Christian contemplatives, as is proved by the case of the Sufi Ibrāhīm ibn Adham, but the most immediate explanation of the kinship between Sufism and Christian monasticism does not lie in historical events. As ʿAbd al-Karīm al-Jīlī explains in his book *Al-Insān al-Kāmil* ("Universal Man") the message of Christ unveils certain inner—and therefore esoteric—aspects of the monotheism of Abraham.

In a certain sense Christian dogmas, which can be all reduced to the dogma of the two natures of Christ, the divine and the human, sum up in a "historical" form all that Sufism teaches on union with God. Moreover, Sufis hold that the Lord Jesus (*Sayyidnā* ʿĪsa) is of all the Divine Envoys (*rusul*) the most perfect type of contemplative saint. To offer the left cheek to him who smites one on the right is true spiritual detachment; it is a voluntary withdrawal from the interplay of cosmic actions and reactions.

It is none the less true that for Sufis the person of Christ does not stand in the same perspective as it does for Christians. Despite many likenesses the Sufi way differs greatly from the way of Christian contemplatives. We may here refer to the picture in which the different traditional ways are depicted as the radii of a circle which are united only at one single point. The nearer the radii are to the center, the nearer they are to one another; none the less they coincide only at the center where they cease to be radii. It is clear that this distinction of one way from another does not prevent the intellect from placing itself by an intuitive anticipation at the center where all ways converge.

To make the inner constitution of Sufism quite clear it should be added that it always includes as indispensable elements, first, a doctrine, secondly, an initiation and, thirdly, a spiritual method. The doctrine is, as it were, a symbolical prefiguring of the knowledge to be attained; it is also, in its manifestation, a fruit of that knowledge.

The quintessence of Sufi doctrine comes from the Prophet, but, as there is no esotericism without a certain inspiration, the doctrine is continually manifested afresh by the mouth of masters. Oral teaching

[3] Certain Sufis deliberately manifested forms which, though not contrary to the spirit of the Tradition, shocked the commonalty of exotericists. This was a way of making themselves free from the psychic elements and mental habits of the collectivity surrounding them.

is moreover superior, since it is direct and "personal", to what can be gleaned from writings. Writings play only a secondary part as a preparation, a complement, or an aid to memory and for this reason the historical continuity of Sufi teaching sometimes eludes the researches of scholars.

As for initiation in Sufism, this consists in the transmission of a spiritual influence (*barakah*) and must be conferred by a representative of a "chain" reaching back to the Prophet. In most cases it is transmitted by the master who also communicates the method and confers the means of spiritual concentration that are appropriate to the aptitudes of the disciple. The general framework of the method is the Islamic Law, although there have always been isolated Sufis who, by reason of the exceptional nature of their contemplative state, no longer took part in the ordinary ritual of Islam.

In order to forestall any objection which might be raised on this account to what had already been said about the Muḥammadan origin of Sufism it must here be clearly stated that the spiritual supports on which the principal methods of Sufism are based, and which can in certain circumstances take the place of the ordinary ritual of Islam, appear as the very keystones of the whole Islamic symbolism; it is indeed this sense that they were given by the Prophet himself.

Initiation generally takes the form of a pact (*bayʿah*) between the candidate and the spiritual master (*al-murshid*) who represents the Prophet. This pact implies perfect submission of the disciple to the master in all that concerns spiritual life and it can never be dissolved unilaterally by the will of the disciple.

The different "branches" of the spiritual "family tree" of Sufism correspond quite naturally to different "paths" (*ṭuruq*). Each great master from whom the start of a specific branch can be traced has authority to adopt the method to the aptitude of a particular category of those who are gifted for spiritual life. Thus the various "paths" correspond to various "vocations" all of them orientated to the same goal, and are in no sense schisms or "sects" within Sufism, although partial deviations have also arisen from time to time and given birth to sects in the strict sense. The outward sign of a sectarian tendency is always the quantitative and "dynamic" manner in which propagation takes place. Authentic Sufism can never become a "movement"[4] for

[4] In some *ṭuruq*, such as the Qādiriyah, the Darqāwiyah, and the Naqshbandiyah, the presence of "outer circles" of initiates in addition to the inner circle of the elite results

the very good reason that it appeals to what is most "static" in man, to wit, contemplative intellect.[5]

In this connection it should be noted that, if Islam has been able to remain intact throughout the centuries despite the changes in human psychology and the ethnic differences between the Islamic peoples, this is assuredly not because of the relatively dynamic character it possesses as a collective form but because from its very origin it includes a possibility of intellectual contemplation which transcends the affective currents of the human soul.

in a certain popular expansion. But this is not to be confounded with the expansion of sectarian movements, since the outer circles do not stand in opposition to exotericism of which they are very often in fact an intensified form.

[5] What is in these days usually called the "intellect" is really only the discursive faculty, the very dynamism and agitation of which distinguishes it from the intellect proper which is in itself motionless being always direct and serene in operation.

Chapter 2

SUFISM AND MYSTICISM

Scientific works commonly define Sufism as "Muslim mysticism" and we too would readily adopt the epithet "mystical" to designate that which distinguishes Sufism from the simply religious aspect of Islam if that word still bore the meaning given it by the Greek Fathers of the early Christian Church and those who followed their spiritual line: they used it to designate what is related to knowledge of "the mysteries". Unfortunately the word "mysticism"—and also the word "mystical"—has been abused and extended to cover religious manifestations which are strongly marked with individualistic subjectivity and governed by a mentality which does not look beyond the horizons of exotericism.

It is true that there are in the East, as in the West, borderline cases such as that of the *majdhūb* in whom the Divine attraction (*al-jadhb*) strongly predominates so as to invalidate the working of the mental faculties with the result that the *majdhūb* cannot give doctrinal formulation to his contemplative state. It may also be that a state of spiritual realization comes about in exceptional cases almost without the support of a regular method, for "the Spirit bloweth whither It listeth". None the less the term *Taṣawwuf* is applied in the Islamic world only to regular contemplative ways which include both an esoteric doctrine and transmission from one master to another. So *Taṣawwuf* could only be translated as "mysticism" on condition that the latter term was explicitly given its strict meaning, which is also its original meaning. If the word were understood in that sense it would clearly be legitimate to compare Sufis to true Christian mystics. All the same a shade of meaning enters here which, while it does not touch the meaning of the word "mysticism" taken by itself, explains why it does not seem satisfactory in all its contexts to transpose it into Sufism. Christian contemplatives, and especially those who came after the Middle Ages, are indeed related to those Muslim contemplatives who followed the way of spiritual love (*al-maḥabbah*), the *bhakti mārga* of Hinduism, but only very rarely are they related to those Eastern contemplatives who were of a purely intellectual order, such as Ibn ʿArabī or, in the Hindu world, Śrī Śaṅkarāchārya.[1]

Now spiritual love is in a sense intermediate between glowing devotion and knowledge; moreover, the language of the *bhakta* projects, even into the realm of final union, the polarity from which love springs. This is no doubt one reason why, in the Christian world, the distinction between true mysticism and individualistic "mysticism" is not always clearly marked, whereas in the world of Islam esotericism always involves a metaphysical view of things—even in its bhaktic forms—and is thus clearly separated from exotericism, which can in this case be much more readily defined as the common "Law".[2]

Every complete way of contemplation, such as the Sufi way or Christian mysticism (in the original meaning of that word), is distinct from a way of devotion, such as is wrongly called "mystical", in that it implies an active intellectual attitude. Such an attitude is by no means to be understood in the sense of a sort of individualism with an intellectual air to it: on the contrary it implies a disposition to open oneself to the essential Reality (*al-ḥaqīqah*), which transcends discursive thought and so also a possibility of placing oneself intellectually beyond all individual subjectivity.

That there may be no misunderstanding about what has just been said it must be clearly stated that the Sufi also realizes an attitude of perpetual adoration molded by the religious form. Like every believer he must pray and, in general, conform to the revealed Law since his individual human nature will always remain passive in relation to Divine Reality or Truth whatever the degree of his spiritual identification with it. "The servant (i.e. the individual) always remains the servant" (*al-ʿabd yabqā-l-ʿabd*), as a Moroccan master said to the author. In this relationship the Divine Presence will therefore manifest Itself as Grace. But the intelligence of the Sufi, inasmuch as it is directly identified with the "Divine Ray", is in a certain manner withdrawn, in its spiritual actuality and its own modes of expression, from the

[1] There is in this fact nothing implying any superiority of one tradition over another; it shows only tendencies which are conditioned by the genius and temperament of the peoples concerned. Because of this bhaktic character of Christian mysticism some orientalists have found it possible to assert that Ibn ʿArabī was "not a real mystic".

[2] The structure of Islam does not admit of stages in some sense intermediate between exotericism and esotericism such as the Christian monastic state, the original role of which was to constitute a direct framework for the Christian way of contemplation.

framework imposed on the individual by religion and also by reason, and in this sense the inner nature of the Sufi is not receptivity but pure act.

It goes without saying that not every contemplative who follows the Sufi way comes to realize a state of knowledge which is beyond form, for clearly that does not depend on his will alone. None the less the end in view not only determines the intellectual horizon but also brings into play spiritual means which, being as it were a prefiguring of that end, permit the contemplative to take up an active position in relation to his own psychic form.

Instead of identifying himself with his empirical "I" he fashions that "I" by virtue of an element which is symbolically and implicitly non-individual. The Qur᾿ān says: "We shall strike vanity with truth and it will bring it to naught" (21:18). The Sufi ʿAbd as-Salām ibn Mashīsh prayed: "Strike with me on vanity that I may bring it to naught." To the extent that he is effectively emancipated the contemplative ceases to be such-and-such a person and "becomes" the Truth on which he has meditated and the Divine Name which he invokes.

The intellectual essence of Sufism makes imprints even on the purely human aspects of the way which may in practice coincide with the religious virtues. In the Sufi perspective the virtues are nothing other than human images or "subjective traces" of universal Truth;[3] hence the incompatibility between the spirit of Sufism and the "moralistic" conception of virtue, which is quantitative and individualistic.[4]

Since the doctrine is both the very foundation of the way and the fruit of the contemplation which is its goal,[5] the difference between Sufism and religious mysticism can be reduced to a question of doctrine. This can be clearly expressed by saying that the believer whose

[3] It will be recalled that for Plotinus virtue is intermediate between the soul and intelligence.

[4] A quantitative conception of virtue results from the religious consideration of merit or even from a purely social point of view. The qualitative conception on the other hand has in view the analogical relation between a cosmic or Divine quality and a human virtue. Of necessity the religious conception of virtue remains individualistic since it values virtue only from the point of view of individual salvation.

[5] Some orientalists would like artificially to separate doctrine from "spiritual experience". They see doctrine as a "conceptualizing" anticipating a purely subjective "experience". They forget two things: first, that the doctrine ensues from a state of knowledge which is the goal of the way and secondly, that God does not lie.

doctrinal outlook is limited to that of exotericism always maintains a fundamental and irreducible separation between the Divinity and himself whereas the Sufi recognizes, at least in principle, the essential unity of all beings, or—to put the same thing in negative terms—the unreality of all that appears separate from God.

It is necessary to keep in view this double aspect of esoteric orientation because it may happen that an exotericist—and particularly a religious mystic—will also affirm that in the sight of God he is nothing. If, however, this affirmation carried with it for him all its metaphysical implications, he would logically be forced to admit at the same time the positive aspect of the same truth, which is that the essence of his own reality, in virtue of which he is *not* "nothing", is mysteriously identical with God. As Meister Eckhart wrote: "There is somewhat in the soul which is uncreate and uncreatable; if all the soul were such it would be uncreate and uncreatable; and this somewhat is Intellect." This is a truth which all esotericism admits *a priori*, whatever the manner in which it is expressed.

A purely religious teaching on the other hand either does not take it into account or even explicitly denies it, because of the danger that the great majority of believers would confuse the Divine Intellect with its human, "created" reflection and would not be able to conceive of their transcendent unity except in the likeness of a substance the quasi-material coherence of which would be contrary to the essential uniqueness of every being. It is true that the Intellect has a "created" aspect both in the human and in the cosmic order, but the whole scope of the meaning that can be given to the word "Intellect"[6] is not what concerns us here since, independently of this question, esotericism is characterized by its affirmation of the essentially divine nature of knowledge.

[6] The doctrine of the Christian contemplatives of the Orthodox Church, though clearly esoteric, maintains an apparently irreducible distinction between the "Uncreated Light" and the *nous* or intellect, which is a human, and so created faculty, created to know that Light. Here the "identity of essence" is expressed by the immanence of the "Uncreated Light" and its presence in the heart. From the point of view of method the distinction between the intellect and Light is a safeguard against a "luciferian" confusion of the intellectual organ with the Divine Intellect. The Divine Intellect immanent in the world may even be conceived as the "void", for the Intellect which "grasps" all cannot itself be "grasped". The intrinsic orthodoxy of this point of view—which is also the Buddhist point of view—is seen in the identification of the essential reality of everything with this "void" (*śūnya*).

Exotericism stands on the level of formal intelligence which is conditioned by its objects, which are partial and mutually exclusive truths. As for esotericism, it realizes that intelligence which is beyond forms and it alone moves freely in its limitless space and sees how relative truths are delimited.[7]

This brings us to a further point which must be made clear, a point, moreover, indirectly connected with the distinction drawn above between true mysticism and individualistic "mysticism". Those who stand "outside" often attribute to Sufis the pretension of being able to attain to God by the sole means of their own will. In truth it is precisely the man whose orientation is towards action and merit—that is, exoteric—who most often tends to look on everything from the point of an effort of will, and from this arises his lack of understanding of the purely contemplative point of view which envisages the way first of all in relation to knowledge.

In the principial order will does in fact depend on knowledge and not vice versa, knowledge being by its nature "impersonal". Although its development, starting from the symbolism transmitted by the traditional teaching, does include a certain logical process, knowledge is none the less a divine gift which man could not take to himself by his own initiative. If this is taken into account it is easier to understand what was said above about the nature of those spiritual means which are strictly "initiatic" and are as it were a prefiguring of the non-human goal of the Way. While every human effort, every effort of the will to get beyond the limitations of individuality is doomed to fall back on itself, those means which are, so to say, of the same nature as the supra-individual Truth (*al-Ḥaqīqah*) which they evoke and prefigure can, and alone can, loosen the knot of microcosmic individuation—the egocentric illusion, as the Vedāntists would say—since only the Truth in its universal and supra-mental reality can consume its opposite without leaving of it any residue.

By comparison with this radical negation of the "I" (*nafs*) any means which spring from the will alone, such as asceticism (*az-zuhd*) can play only a preparatory and ancillary part.[8] It may be added that it

[7] The Qur'ān says: "God created the Heavens and the earth by the Truth (*al-Ḥaqq*)" (64:3).

[8] Sufis see in the body not only the soil which nourishes the passions but also its spiritually positive aspect which is that of a picture or résumé of the cosmos. In Sufi writings the expression the "temple" (*haykal*) will be found to designate the body.

is for this reason that such means never acquired in Sufism the almost absolute importance they had, for instance, for certain Christian monks; and this is true even in cases where they were in fact strictly practiced in one or another *ṭarīqah*.

A Sufi symbolism which has the advantage of lying outside the realm of any psychological analysis will serve to sum up what has just been said. The picture it gives is this: The Spirit (*ar-Rūḥ*) and the soul (*an-nafs*) engage in battle for the possession of their common son the heart (*al-qalb*). By *ar-Rūḥ* is here to be understood the intellectual principle which transcends the individual nature[9] and by *an-nafs* the psyche, the centrifugal tendencies of which determine the diffuse and inconstant domain of the "I". As for *al-qalb*, the heart, this represents the central organ of the soul, corresponding to the vital center of the physical organism. *Al-qalb* is in a sense the point of intersection of the "vertical" ray, which is *ar-Rūḥ*, with the "horizontal" plane, which is *an-nafs*.

Now it is said that the heart takes on the nature of that one of the two elements generating it which gains the victory in this battle. Inasmuch as the *nafs* has the upper hand the heart is "veiled" by her, for the soul, which takes herself to be an autonomous whole, in a way envelops it in her "veil" (*ḥijāb*). At the same time the *nafs* is an accomplice of the "world" in its multiple and changing aspect because she passively espouses the cosmic condition of form. Now form divides and binds whereas the Spirit, which is above form, unites and at the same time distinguishes reality from appearance. If, on the contrary, the Spirit gains the victory over the soul, then the heart will be transformed into Spirit and will at the same time transmute the soul suffusing her with spiritual light. Then too the heart reveals itself as what it really is, that is as the tabernacle (*mishkāh*) of the Divine Mystery (*sirr*) in man.

In this picture the Spirit appears with a masculine function in relation to the soul, which is feminine. But the Spirit is receptive and so feminine in its turn in relation to the Supreme Being, from which it is, however, distinguished only by its cosmic character inasmuch as it is polarized with respect to created beings. In essence *ar-Rūḥ* is identi-

Muḥyi-d-Dīn ibn ʿArabī in the chapter on Moses in his *Fuṣūṣ al-Ḥikam* compares it to "the ark where dwells the Peace (*Sakīnah*) of the Lord".

[9] The word *rūḥ* can also have a more particular meaning, that of "vital spirit". This is the sense in which it is most frequently used in cosmology.

fied with the Divine Act or Order (*al-Amr*) which is symbolized in the Qur'ān by the creating Word "Be" (*kun*) and is the immediate and eternal "enunciation" of the Supreme Being: ". . . and they will question you about the Spirit: say: The Spirit is of the Order of my Lord, but you have received but little knowledge" (Qur'ān, 17:85).

In the process of his spiritual liberation the contemplative is reintegrated into the Spirit and by It into the primordial enunciation of God by which "all things were made . . . and nothing that was made was made without it" (St. John's Gospel, 1:3).[10] Moreover, the name "Sufi" means, strictly speaking, one who is essentially identified with the Divine Act; hence the saying that the "Sufi is not created" (*aṣ-ṣufi lam yukhlaq*), which can also be understood as meaning that the being who is thus reintegrated into the Divine Reality recognizes himself in it "such as he was" from all eternity according to his "principial possibility, immutable in its state of non-manifestation"—to quote Muḥyi-d-Dīn ibn 'Arabī. Then all his created modalities are revealed, whether they are temporal or nontemporal, as mere inconsistent reflections of this principial possibility.[11]

[10] For the Alexandrines too liberation is brought about in three stages which respectively correspond to the Holy Spirit, the Word, and God the Father.

[11] If it is legitimate to speak of the principial, or divine, possibility of every being, this possibility being the very reason for his "personal uniqueness", it does not follow from this that there is any multiplicity whatever in the divine order, for there cannot be any uniqueness outside the Divine Unity. This truth is a paradox only on the level of discursive reason. It is hard to conceive only because we almost inevitably forge for ourselves a "substantial" picture of the Divine Unity.

Chapter 3

SUFISM AND PANTHEISM

All the metaphysical doctrines of the East and some of those of the West have frequently been labeled as pantheistic, but in truth pantheism is only to be found in the case of certain European philosophers and in some Orientals who were influenced by Western thought of the nineteenth century. Pantheism arose from the same mental tendency which produced, first, naturalism and then materialism. Pantheism only conceives of the relationship between the Divine Principle and things from the one point of view of substantial or existential continuity, and this is an error explicitly rejected by every traditional doctrine.

If there were such a continuity by virtue of which God and the manifested universe could be compared as a branch can be compared with the trunk from which it sprang, then this continuity, or (what amounts to the same thing) the substance common to the two terms, would either be determined by some superior principle which differentiated it or would itself be superior to the two terms which it bound together and, in a sense, included: God would then not be God. Now it might he said that God is Himself this continuity, or this Unity, but in that case it would not be conceived of as outside Him, so that He is in reality beyond compare and therefore distinct from everything manifested, but without the possibility of anything being "outside" or "beside" Him.

Now, as Muḥyi-d-Dīn ibn ʿArabī says in his "Epistle on Unity", the *Risālat al-Aḥadīyah*:

> . . . None grasps Him save He Himself. None knows Him but He Himself. . . . He knows Himself by Himself. . . . Other-than-He cannot grasp Him. His impenetrable veil is His own Oneness. Other-than-He does not cloak Him. His veil is His very existence. He is veiled by His Oneness in a manner that cannot be explained. Other-than-He does not see Him; whether prophet, envoy, or perfected saint, or angel near unto Him. His prophet is He Himself. His envoy is He. His message is He. His word is He. He has sent word of His Ipseity

> by Himself, from Himself to Himself, without intermediary or causality other than Himself. . . . Other-than-He has no existence and so cannot bring itself to naught. . . .

Now, if it happens that masters of esotericism make use of the picture of a material continuity in order to express the essential Unity of things, just as when Hindu advaitins compare things to pots of differing form but all made of clay, they are perfectly well aware of the inadequacy of such a picture. Moreover, this quite evident inadequacy excludes the danger of people reading into it anything more than a symbolic allusion. As for the allusion itself, its whole justification is based on the inverse analogy which exists between the essential unity of things—all of them "made of Knowledge"—and their "material" unity, which has nothing to do with any theory of "causality" in the cosmological sense of that word.

Again, it must be added that the contemplative never tends to enclose reality in any single one of its modes—such as substantial continuity—or in any single one of its levels—such as sensory existence or intelligible existence—to the exclusion of others. On the contrary, he recognizes innumerable levels of reality, the hierarchy of which is irreversible, so that one can affirm of the relative that it is in essence one with its principle,[1] or that it "is" its principle, although one cannot say of the principle that it is included in its product. Thus, all beings are God, if considered in their essential reality, but God is not these beings and this, not in the sense that His reality excludes them, but because in the face of His infinity their reality is nil.

The essential Unity (*al-Aḥadīyah*), in which all diversity is "drowned" or "extinguished", is in no wise contradicted by the metaphysical idea of the indefinite number of levels or degrees of existence. On the contrary, these two truths are intimately connected one with the other. This is clear as soon as the Divine Infinity (*al-Kamāl*) is envisaged "through" each of them—inasmuch as the Infinite can be "envisaged". Then—to speak figuratively—the Infinite either "comprises" or "dilates" according to whether it is envisaged in its principial determination, which is Unity, or its cosmic reflection, which is the inexhaustible and indefinite nature of existence.

[1] By the word "principle" is here to be understood the ontological cause, independent of its effects.

This enables us to understand that the Sufi doctrine of Unity (which is strictly analogous, despite the difference in terminology, to the Hindu advaitic doctrine of "Non-Duality"), has no connection with a philosophical "monism", as modern critics of such Sufi *jñānins* as Ibn 'Arabī or 'Abd al-Karīm al-Jīlī try to pretend. Their opinion is the more astounding since the doctrinal method of these masters consists in bringing out extreme ontological contrasts and envisaging the essential Unity not by rational reduction but by an intuitive integration of paradox.[2]

[2] According to the expression of Sahl at-Tustarī: "One knows God by the Union of the contrary (qualities) which relate to Him."

Chapter 4

KNOWLEDGE AND LOVE

It is characteristic of Sufism that its expressions often hold the balance between love and knowledge. An emotional form of expression more easily integrates the religious attitude which is the starting point of all Islamic spirituality. The language of love makes it possible to enunciate the most profoundly esoteric truths without coming into conflict with dogmatic theology. Finally, the intoxication of love symbolically corresponds to states of knowledge which go beyond discursive thought.

There are also expressions which, though they do not arise from an attitude of love, none the less evoke love because they reflect an inner beauty which is the seal set by Unity on the soul. It is from this Unity that clarity and rhythm spring, whereas any kind of mental crispation and vanity of speech contradicts the simplicity and so also the transparence of the soul in relation to Truth.

Some Sufi writers, such as Muḥyi-d-Dīn ibn ʿArabī, Aḥmad ibn al ʿArīf, Suhrawardī of Aleppo, al-Junayd, and Abu-l-Ḥasan ash-Shādhilī give evidence of an attitude which is fundamentally intellectual. These writers look on the Divine Reality as the universal essence of all knowledge. Others, such as ʿOmar ibn al-Fārid, Manṣūr al-Ḥallāj, and Jalāl ad-Dīn Rūmī, express themselves in the language of love. For them the Divine Reality is, first of all, the limitless object of desire. But this diversity of attitude has nothing to do with any divergence between different schools, as some have believed who consider that the Sufis who used an intellectual language had been affected by the influence of doctrines foreign to Islam such as Neoplatonism, and that only those who represent an emotional attitude are the mouthpiece of the true mysticism which derives from the perspective of monotheism.

In fact the diversity in question derives from a diversity of vocation: different vocations quite naturally graft themselves on to different types of human genius and all find their place in true *taṣawwuf*; the difference between an intellectual and an emotional attitude is merely the most important and the commonest of the differences that are to be found in this domain.

Hinduism, which is characterized by an extreme differentiation of spiritual methods, makes an explicit distinction between the three ways of knowledge (*jñāna*), love (*bhakti*), and action (*karma*). This distinction is in fact to be found in every complete tradition. In Sufism the distinction of the three ways corresponds to the three main motives of aspiration towards God—knowledge or gnosis (*al-maʿrifah*), love (*al-maḥabbah*), and fear (*al-khawf*). But Sufism tends rather to synthesis than to differentiation of these ways and in fact in "classical" Sufism a certain equilibrium of the intellectual and emotional attitudes is noticeable. Doubtless the reason for this lies in the general structure of Islam which is founded on *at-tawḥīd*, the doctrine of Unity, and so gives an intellectual orientation which is imposed on all varieties of the spiritual life. As for love, love is born spontaneously wherever the Divine Reality is felt or contemplated.

This brings us back to the opinion that only those Sufis who manifest an attitude of love truly represent the mystical aspect of Islam. In support of this opinion criteria are wrongly applied which are valid only in relation to Christianity, the basic theme of which is Divine Love so that those who are the mouthpieces of gnosis in Christianity express themselves—though there are some rare exceptions—through the symbolism of love.

This is not the case in Islam where at every level knowledge takes unquestioned precedence.[1] Moreover, true knowledge or gnosis in no way implies an emphasis on the mind at the expense of the emotional faculties: its organ is the heart, the secret and ungraspable center of man's being, and the radiations of knowledge penetrate into the whole sphere of the soul. A Sufi who has realized utterly "impersonal" knowledge may none the less make use of the language of love and reject all doctrinal dialectic; in such a case the intoxication of love will correspond to states of knowledge which are beyond forms and outstrip all thought.

In reality the distinction between the way of knowledge and the way of love amounts to a question of the predominance of one or the other; there is never in fact a complete separation between these two

[1] It may be noted in passing that, if Muḥyi-d-Dīn ibn ʿArabī gives a more universal meaning to the word *ʿilm*, which is also translated as "Knowledge", than to *maʿrifah*, that is because in Islamic theology the former corresponds to a Divine attribute. *Al-maʿrifah* is an incidental participation in Divine Knowledge and could be translated as "gnosis", in the sense in which that word was used by Clement of Alexandria.

modes of spirituality. Knowledge of God always engenders love, while love presupposes knowledge of the object of love even though that knowledge may be only indirect and reflected. The object of spiritual love is Divine Beauty, which is an aspect of Infinity, and through this object desire becomes lucid or clear. Full, integral love, which revolves round a single ineffable point, gives a sort of subjective infallibility.

By this we mean that its infallibility does not apply to universal and "objective" truths, as does the infallibility that comes from knowledge, but only to all that forms part of the "personal" relationship of the adorer to his Lord. It is in the object, Beauty, that love virtually coincides with knowledge. In a sense Truth and Beauty are criteria of one another, although sentimental prejudices distort the concept of beauty just as, from another angle, rationalism limits truth.

It is highly significant that there is hardly a single Muslim metaphysician who did not compose poetry and whose most abstract prose is not in some passages transformed into rhythmic language full of poetic images, while, on the other hand, the poetry of the most famous hymners of love, such as ʿUmar ibn al-Fārid and Jalāl ad-Dīn Rūmī, is rich in intellectual perceptions.

As for the attitude of fear (*al-khawf*), which corresponds to the way of action, this is not directly manifested in the style of expression; its role is an implicit one. It is true that fear stands, as it were, only at the threshold of contemplation, but, when it is spiritualized, it can none the less bring man out of the collective dream which the "world" is and bring him face to face with Eternal Reality. Love is higher than fear even as knowledge is higher than love, but this is true only of direct, immediate knowledge which outstrips reason (or discursive thought), for spiritual love embraces every individual faculty and imprints each of them with the seal of Unity.[2]

In his *Maḥāsin al-Majālis* Aḥmad ibn al-ʿArīf says that love (*al-maḥabbah*) is "the beginning of the valleys of extinction (*fanāʾ*) and the hill from which there is a descent towards the stages of self-naughting (*al-maḥū*); it is the last of the stages where the advance guard of the mass of believers meets the rear guard of the elect". Muḥyi-d-Dīn ibn ʿArabī on the other hand considers love to be the highest station of the soul and subordinates to it every possible human perfection.

[2] On the question of knowledge and love and the distinction between the ways corresponding to these see Frithjof Schuon, *Spiritual Perspectives and Human Facts* (London: Perennial Books, 1970).

This may seem strange, coming as it does from one of the most eminent of the representatives of the way of knowledge. The explanation is that, for Ibn ʿArabī , knowledge is not a station of the soul. In the perfection of knowledge nothing specifically human remains since such knowledge is identified with its object, the Divine Reality. In its immediate actuality knowledge can thus no longer be attributed to man or to the soul but only to God, since it no longer has any psychic outline. At the same time the most lofty station of the soul is not a psychological correlative of knowledge like prudence or veracity but is integral love, the complete absorption of the human will by the Divine attraction. It is the state of being "lost in love" of which Abraham is the human prototype. (Cf. Ibn ʿArabī: *Fuṣūṣ al-Ḥikam.*)

Chapter 5

THE BRANCHES OF THE DOCTRINE

Not being a philosophy, that is, a merely human mode of thought, Sufi doctrine is not presented as the homogeneous development of a mental point of view. Of necessity it includes many points of view which may on occasions be mutually contradictory, if their logical form is alone taken into account without regard to the universal truth to which they all relate. Because of this it may be that one master rejects some doctrinal assertion of another master whose authority he none the less recognizes.

Thus, for example, ʿAbd al-Karīm al-Jīlī, in his book *Al-Insān al-Kāmil* (Universal Man) which is founded on the teaching of Ibn ʿArabī, rejects the latter's statement that Divine Knowledge depends, like every science, on its object. He does so because this statement could lead to a belief that Divine Knowledge is dependent on what is relative. Now Ibn ʿArabī refers Divine Knowledge to the pure possibilities principially contained in the Divine Essence, so that the apparent duality between Knowledge and its object does not exist except in the terminology, and the dependence of which he speaks is no more than a logical picture of the principial identity of the possible and the real.[1]

Sufi doctrine includes several branches in which two chief domains can be distinguished, that of Universal Truths (*al-Haqāʾiq*) and that which relates to human and individual stages of the way (*ad-daqāʾiq*) or, in other words, metaphysic and a "science of the soul". Needless to say these domains are not separated into watertight compartments. Metaphysic includes everything, but in Sufism it is always envisaged according to points of view connected with spiritual realization. The cosmology is derived from metaphysic and applied at the same time to the macrocosm and to the microcosm, so that there is a psychology

[1] In the same way, according to Origen, the Divine foreknowledge relates to pure possibilities: it includes possibilities but does not determine them, and that is why Divine foreknowledge and human free-will are not mutually exclusive. Cf. *The Philokalia of Origen* on the subject of destiny.

of cosmic amplitude just as there is a cosmology built up on analogy with the inner constitution of man.

In order to put this quite clearly it is necessary to insist at some length on this relationship. Apart from the two domains of *al-Haqā'iq* and *ad-daqā'iq* already mentioned, three chief domains of doctrine can be distinguished—metaphysic, cosmology, and spiritual psychology. This distinction corresponds to the triad: God, the world (or the macrocosm), and the soul (or microcosm). In its turn cosmology can be conceived either by applying metaphysical principles to the cosmos—and this is the contemplation of God in the world—or by drawing an analogy between the cosmos and the human soul.

Moreover in its complete development cosmology necessarily includes the cosmic reality of the soul, while no spiritual psychology can cut off the soul from cosmic principles. In the fabric of the cosmos there is no radical break. In its own fashion discontinuity does exist; it is what it is. But discontinuity is barely conceivable apart from a principle of unity which bridges the gap and without the background of a continuity which manifests it. Thus, for instance, the apparent discontinuity between individuals, the relation of their respective centers of consciousness, is only the mark of their unique Essence which "vertically" transcends the "horizontal" plane of their common nature.

As for the discontinuity between individual consciousness in general and the levels of Intelligence which are beyond form, it exists in terms of the quasi-material level of consciousness which links it "horizontally" with other consciousnesses that are on the level of form but at the same time also separates it from their unique Essence.

Thus reality is regarded according to different orders of continuity depending upon the point of view adopted or imposed on us by the very nature of things, and metaphysic alone can embrace all these various perspectives and give to them their proper place in that web of visions, the universe.

In itself cosmology is an analytical science in the original meaning of that term, for it reduces every aspect of the cosmos to the underlying principles, which are, in the last analysis, the active and the passive poles, the "informing" principle that molds and the plastic substance or *materia prima*. The integration of these complementary principles in the primary Unity belongs to the realm of metaphysic and not to cosmology.

It has just been stated that Sufi psychology does not separate the soul either from the metaphysical or from the cosmic order. The connection with the metaphysical order provides spiritual psychology with qualitative criteria such as are wholly lacking in profane psychology, which studies only the dynamic character of phenomena of the psyche and their proximate causes. When modern psychology makes pretensions to a sort of science of the hidden contents of the soul it is still for all that restricted to an individual perspective because it has no real means for distinguishing psychic forms which translate universal realities from forms which appear symbolical but are only the vehicles for individual impulsions. Its "collective subconscious" has most assuredly nothing to do with the true source of symbols; at most it is a chaotic depositary of psychic residues somewhat like the mud of the ocean bed which retains traces of past epochs.

For profane psychology the only link between the macrocosm and the world of the soul lies in the impressions which reach the soul through the gateway of the senses, but Sufi psychology takes account of the analogy in constitution between the macrocosm and the human microcosm. To this order of ideas belong such sciences as astrology, the symbolism of which has been used incidentally by certain Sufi masters.

The Sufi path can be considered as a way towards knowledge of oneself in conformity with the saying of the Prophet: "He who knows himself (*nafsahu*) knows his Lord". It is true that this knowledge applies ultimately to the Unique Essence, the immutable Self (*al-huwiyah*) and so goes beyond any cosmological or psychological perspective, but, at a relative level, in so far as it concerns one's individual nature, knowledge of oneself necessarily includes a science of the soul. To a certain extent this science is a cosmology; above all it is a discrimination as regards the motives of the soul.

To show how discrimination of the soul is inspired by cosmological principles, certain very general criteria of inspiration (*al-wārid*) may be cited by way of illustration. It must, however, first be made clear that inspiration is here taken, not in the sense of prophetic inspiration, but in the sense of the sudden intuition normally provoked by spiritual practices. This inspiration may have very different sources, but is valid only when it comes from the center of man's being outside time or from the "Angel", in other words from the ray of Universal Intelligence connecting man to God.

It is deceptive when it is derived from the psychic world, whether it comes on the one hand from the individual psyche, or the subtle medium in which the psyche lives, or, on the other hand, through the human psyche from the sub-human world and its satanic pole. Inspiration which comes from the Angel, and so implicitly from God, always communicates a new perception which illuminates the "I" and at the same time relativizes it by dissolving certain of its illusions. When inspiration comes from the individual psyche it speaks for some hidden passion and so has something egocentric about it and is accompanied by some direct or indirect pretentiousness. As for inspirations which emanate from the satanic pole, these go so far as to invert hierarchical relationships and to deny higher realities.

Impulsions which come from the individual or collective soul insist tirelessly on the same object—the object of some desire—whereas the satanic influence only makes use provisionally of some lure of passion: what it really seeks is not the object of the passion but the implicit negation of a spiritual reality; that is why the devil routs discussion by changing his "theme" every time his argument is destroyed. He argues only to trouble man whereas the passional soul has a certain logical consecutiveness so that its impulsions can be directed into legitimate channels by dint of sufficiently decisive arguments, whereas satanic impulsions must simply be rejected *in toto*. The three tendencies in question respectively correspond to reintegration into the Essence, to a centrifugal dispersion, and to a "fall" into sub-human chaos, and they have their analogies in the universal order. Hinduism calls them *sattva*, *rajas*, and *tamas*.

It may be surprising that so many Sufi books treat of the virtues when Knowledge (*al-ma'rifah*) is the only goal of the way and perpetual concentration on God the sole condition needed for arriving at it. If the virtues can certainly not be neglected, it is precisely because no mode of consciousness can he regarded as being outside total Knowledge—or outside Truth—nor any inner attitude as being indifferent. "Sight of the heart" (*ru'yat al-qalb*) is a knowledge of the whole being. It is impossible for the heart to open up to Divine Truth so long as the soul retains, in point of fact if not consciously, an attitude which denies that Truth, and avoidance of this is the more uncertain since the domain of the soul (*an-nafs*) is *a priori* governed by the egocentric illusion which itself presupposes a blind spot.[2] All this amounts to saying that the science of the virtues, which applies Divine Truth to the

[2] All the same man always has a certain awareness of the falsity of his attitude, even if his reason does not take account of it. It is said in the Qur'ān: "Assuredly man is conscious of himself (or: of his own soul) even if he offers excuses" (75:14-15). The

soul, directly concerns spiritual realization. Its criteria are exceedingly subtle; it could never be summed up in a moral code and its fixations are no more than paradigms. Its object, which is spiritual virtue, is a sort of "symbol that is lived", the right perception of which depends on a certain inner development. Now this is not necessarily true of doctrinal understanding.

In a certain sense the Sufi method consists in the art of keeping the soul open to the inflow of the Infinite. Now the soul has a natural tendency to remain shut up in itself and this tendency can be compensated only by a contrary movement acting on the same plane; this movement is precisely virtue. Metaphysical Truth as such is impersonal and motionless; virtue translates it into a "personal" mode.

Spiritual virtue is not necessarily a social virtue in a direct sense, and the external manifestations of one and the same virtue may be different according to the point of view of the circumstances. Thus certain Sufis have shown their contempt for the world by wearing poor and tattered garments; others have affirmed the same inner attitude by wearing sumptuous raiment. In such a Sufi the affirmation of his person is in reality only a submission to the impersonal truth he incarnates; his humility lies in his extinction in an aspect of glory which is not his own.

If Sufi virtue coincides in its form with religious virtue, it none the less differs from it in its contemplative essence. For instance, the virtue of gratitude is, for the mass of believers, founded on the memory of benefits received from God; it implies a feeling that these benefits are more real than the sufferings undergone. In the case of the contemplative this feeling gives place to certainty: for him the plenitude of Being present in every fragment of existence is infinitely more real than the limits of things, and some Sufis have gone so far as to feel joy in what would be for others only a painful negation of themselves.

The spiritual virtues are, as it were, supports in man for the Divine Truth (*al-Ḥaqīqah*); they are also reflections of that Truth. Now any reflection implies a certain inversion in relation to its source: spiritual poverty (*al-faqr*) is, for example, the inverse reflection of the Plenitude of the Spirit. Sincerity (*al-ikhlāṣ*) and veracity (*aṣ-ṣidq*) are expressions of the independence of the spirit from psychic tendencies, while nobility (*al-karam*) is a human reflection of the Divine

man who desires to realize Divine Knowledge while despising virtue is like a robber wanting to become righteous without restoring the product of his robbery.

Grandeur.[3] In these "positive" virtues the inversion lies in the mode and not in the content, which means that they are, as it were, saturated with humility while their prototypes are made of majesty and glory.

[3] One of the most profound works written on the subject of spiritual virtues is the *Maḥāsin al-Majālis* of Ibn al-ʿArīf.

Chapter 6

SUFI INTERPRETATION OF THE QUR'ĀN

Since Sufism represents the inner aspect of Islam its doctrine is in substance an esoteric commentary on the Qur'ān. Now the Prophet himself gave the key to all Qur'ānic exegesis in teachings he gave orally which are verified by the concordance of the chains of intermediaries.[1] Among these sayings of the Prophet some are fundamental for Sufism and they are those which the Prophet enunciated, not as a law-giver, but as a contemplative saint, sayings which were addressed to those of his companions who later became the first Sufi masters. There are also the "holy utterances" (*aḥādīth qudsīyah*) in which God speaks in the first person by the mouth of the Prophet. These latter have the same degree of inspiration as the Qur'ān, though not the same "objective" mode of revelation, and in the main they set forth truths not intended for the whole religious community but only for contemplatives. This is the basis of the Sufi interpretation of the Qur'ān.

As the Prophet stated, the Qur'ān contains in each part several meanings.[2] This is a characteristic common to all revealed texts because the process of revelation in a way repeats the process of divine manifestation, which equally implies a number of levels. The

[1] Certain "specialists" in judging the authenticity of the *aḥādīth* of the Prophet suppose that they can establish the following criteria, disregarding thirteen centuries of Muslim scholarship. They are these: (1) If some *ḥadīth* can be interpreted as favoring some particular group or school, this means it has certainly been invented. If, for instance, it is in favor of the spiritual life, then the Sufis invented it: if on the contrary it provides an argument for literalists hostile to spirituality, then the literalists fabricated it. (2) The more complete the chain of intermediaries indicated by traditionalists, the greater the chance that the particular *ḥadīth* is false because, say they, the need of proof grows in proportion to the lapse of time. Such arguments are truly diabolical for, taken as a whole, they amount to this reasoning: if you bring me no proof it is because you are wrong, but if you do bring proof it means you need it and so again you are wrong. How can these orientalists believe that countless Muslim learned men—men who feared God and hell—could have deliberately fabricated sayings of the Prophet? It would lead one to suppose bad faith to be the most natural thing in the world were it not that "specialists" have almost no feeling for psychological incompatibilities.

[2] According to a saying of the Prophet, "no verse of the Qur'ān has been revealed which has not an external aspect and an inner aspect. Every letter has its definite sense (*ḥadd*) and every definition implies a place of ascent (*maṭla'*)."

interpretation of the "inner" meanings of the Qur᾽ān is founded both on the symbolical nature of the things mentioned and on the multiple meanings of the words. Every language which is relatively primordial, like Arabic, Hebrew, or Sanskrit, has a synthetic character, a verbal expression still implying all the modes of an idea from the concrete up to the universal.[3]

It might be said that the ordinary exegesis of the Qur᾽ān takes the expressions in their immediate meanings whereas the Sufi exegesis uncovers their transposed meanings, or, again, that while exotericism understands them conventionally the Sufi interpretation conceives their direct, original, and spiritually necessary character. When, for example, the Qur᾽ān says that he who accepts God's guidance will be guided "for himself" (*linafsihi*) and that he who remains ignorant is so "on himself" (*῾ala nafsihi*) (see Qur᾽ān, 17:15 and also 4:105) the exoteric interpretation is limited to the idea of the recompense and punishment. The Sufi understands this verse of the Qur᾽ān in the sense of the sayings of the Prophet: "He who knows himself (*nafsahu*) knows his Lord."[4]

The latter interpretation is no less faithful to the literal meaning than is the exoteric interpretation, and indeed it brings out the whole logical strictness of the formula, though without excluding the application envisaged by the learned men "of the exterior" (*῾Ulamā᾽ aẓ-ẓāhir*). In the same way, when the Qur᾽ān affirms that the creation of the heavens and the earth and all creatures was, for God, like the "creation of a single soul", the exoteric interpretation will at most see here the simultaneity of the whole creation where the esoteric interpretation at the same time also deduces from it the intrinsic unity of the cosmos, which is constituted as a single universal being. At times the Sufi exegesis in a sense reverses the exoteric meaning of the text. Thus, the Divine warnings of destruction and annihilation, which are "from the outside" applied to the damned, are incidentally interpreted as describing the self-examination and extinction of the soul in spiri-

[3] This polyvalence of expression has, further, its analogy in the representational art of "archaic" civilizations where the representation of an object may at the same time designate a concrete object, a general idea, and a universal principle.

[4] This interpretation is further confirmed by the context of the passage quoted from the Qur᾽ān. Thus, when it is said that on the day of resurrection man will receive an open book: "Read thy book; it sufficeth that thou shouldest this day make up thine own account" (17:14), the Last Judgment is presented as a knowledge of oneself with regard to which man's will is entirely passive.

tual realization. Indeed the point of view proper to the individuality as such and the point of view of transcendent, impersonal intellect may contradict one another by the very fact of their opposition, which is real though not absolute.

Finally there is the exegesis founded on the phonetic symbolism of the Qur'ān. According to this science each letter—i.e. each sound, since Arabic writing is phonetic—corresponds to a determination of primordial and undifferentiated sound, which is itself like the substance of the perpetual Divine enunciation. Modern Europeans have difficulty in conceiving that a sacred text, though clearly linked with certain historical contingencies, corresponds, even in the very form of its sounds, to realities of a supra-individual order. It will therefore be as well to give here a brief summary of the theory of the revelation of the Qur'ān.

According to the "inner meaning" of the *Sūrat al-Qadr* (97) the Qur'ān "descended" as a whole during the "night of predestination" as an undifferentiated state of Divine knowledge and was "fixed", not in the mind of the Prophet, but in his body, i.e. in the mode of consciousness identified with the body, the relatively undifferentiated nature of which is related to pure cosmic potentiality.[5] Always potentiality is "night" because it contains the possibilities of manifestation in a total way. In the same way the state of perfect receptivity—the state of the Prophet when the Qur'ān "descended"—is a "night" into which no distinctive knowledge penetrates: manifestation is here compared to day. This state is also "peace" because of the Divine Presence which comprehends in their immutable plenitude all the first realities of things—all the Divine "commands".

> In truth, We (God) have made it (the Qur'ān) to descend in the night of predestination.

[5] René Guénon wrote thus of the "night of predestination", the *lailatu'l-qadr*, in which the descent (*tanzīl*) of the Qur'ān took place: ". . . This night, according to the commentary of Muḥyī-d-Dīn ibn 'Arabī, is identified with the very body of the Prophet. What should be particularly noted here is that the 'revelation' was received, not in the mind, but in the body of the being entrusted with the mission of expressing the Principle. The Gospel also says: *Et verbum caro factum est* ('And the Word was made flesh') (*caro* and not *mens*) and this is another and a very exact expression, in the form proper to the Christian tradition, of what the *lailatu'l-qadr* represents in the Islamic tradition" (translated from "Les Deux Nuits", in *Études Traditionnelles*, April and May 1939).

And what shall teach you what is the night of predestination (since reason cannot conceive it)?
The night of predestination is better than a thousand months (that is, better than an indefinite duration);
(In that night) the Angels and the Spirit (*ar-Rūḥ*) descend with the permission (or the full authority) of their Lord for every commandment (*amr*) (to regulate all things).
It is peace, even till the coming of dawn. (Qur'ān, 97)

The state of total knowledge, which was hidden in the "night of predestination" unfathomable by thought, was later translated into words as external events actualized one or another aspect of it, and thus arises the fragmentation of the text into a great many parts and also the repetition, with ever new variations, of the same essential truths which are both simple and rationally inexhaustible. Moreover, this translation into words was made through a cosmic necessity, just as the lightning flashes from supersaturated clouds, and without any discursive elaboration, and this gives the form its direct character not only as regards the mental picture but also in the very sound of the phrases, in which the spiritual power which made them ring out still vibrates.

In order to prevent any misunderstanding, it must again be emphasized that this has no connection with certain modern speculations about an unconscious source from which a psychic impulse arises. What is here called cosmic, in the traditional meaning of that word, in no wise implies the unconscious, at any rate as regards the principle which brings about such a "descent".[6] Moreover, the traditional theory of the revelation of the Qur'ān is in essence the same as that of the revelation of the Veda in Hinduism. The Veda, like the Qur'ān, subsists from all eternity in the Divine Intellect and its "descent" is brought about by virtue of the primordiality of sound. The *rishis*, like the prophets, received it by inspiration, visual and auditory, and transmitted it just as they had seen and heard it without any mental discrimination on their part.

[6] Revelation is "supernatural" because it is divine, but in another relationship it is also "natural". Even in the sensory domain there are events which, though they are natural, break its "normal" continuity and are like images of revelation. Lightning has already been mentioned; snow also is an image of a divine "descent" that transfigures the world and wipes out its impurities, expressing not so much inspiration as a state of sanctity.

In this connection it may be pertinent to refer to another Hindu theory concerning revelation which can also help us to understand certain characteristics of the Qur'ān. Since the revealed text has for its aim nothing but the knowledge of God, the things of this world which it cites by way of example or parable must be understood according to ordinary experience, that is according to the collective subjectivity of mankind, and not as the objects of a scientific statement.[7]

At first sight metaphysical commentary on the Qur'ān seems to be intellectually superior to the text itself for the simple reason that the language of the Qur'ān is religious in form and so linked to human emotionality and to the anthropomorphism of the imagination, whereas the commentary directly sets forth universal truths. But the exegesis suffers from the disadvantages of abstract expression while the sacred text possesses the advantage of the concrete symbol, that is, the synthetic nature in which a single succinct form includes meanings indefinite in their variety.

Sufi commentators know that the anthropomorphic and, so to say, ingenuous form of the sacred text not only answers to a practical need—that of being accessible to the whole of a human collectivity and so to every man,[8] but also corresponds at the same time to the

[7] For instance, when a sacred book like the Qur'ān mentions the motion of the stars, it does so from a geocentric point of view because this perspective is natural to man and is also directly symbolic inasmuch as man's predestined place is at the center of the cosmos.

[8] "The books revealed as a common law (*sharī'ah*) use in speaking of God such expressions that the majority of men grasp their most proximate meaning, whereas the elite understand all their meanings, to wit every meaning implied by each saying according to the rules of the language used" (Muḥyi-d-Dīn ibn 'Arabī in the chapter on Noah of his *Fuṣūṣ al-Ḥikam*). "The prophets use concrete language because they are addressing the collectivity and rely on the understanding of the wise who hear them. If they speak figuratively it is because of the commonalty and because they know the level of intuition of those who truly understand. . . . All that the prophets brought of sciences is clothed in forms accessible to the most ordinary intellectual capacities in order that he who does not go to the bottom of things should stop at this clothing and take it for all that is most beautiful, whereas the man of subtle understanding, the diver who fishes up the pearls of Wisdom, can indicate why this or that (Divine) Truth should be clothed with such and such a terrestrial form. . . . Since the prophets, the Divine messengers (*rusul*), and their (spiritual) heirs know that in the world and in their communities there are men possessing this intuition they rely in their demonstrations on concrete language, accessible both to the elite and to the commonalty; thus one of the elite draws from it at the same time both what the commonalty draw from it and more besides. . ." (ibid., in the chapter on Moses).

process of Divine Manifestation in the sense that the Divine Spirit loves as it were to clothe Itself in concrete forms that are simple and not discursive; herein lies an aspect of the incommensurability of God, who—as the Qur'ān puts it—"is not ashamed to take a gnat as a symbol".[9] This means that the limitation inherent in the symbol cannot lower Him Who is symbolized: on the contrary, it is precisely in virtue of His perfection—or His infinity—that He is reflected at every possible level of existence by "signs" that are always unique.

According to the Prophet all that is contained in the revealed books is to be found in the Qur'ān and all that is contained in the Qur'ān is summed up in the *Sūrat al-Fātiḥah* ("The opening one") while this is in its turn contained in the formula *bismillāhi-r-Raḥmāni-r-Raḥīm* ("In the Name of God, the Compassionate, the Merciful"). This *Sūrat al-Fātiḥah* constitutes the chief text of the ritual prayer; as for the formula, commonly called the *basmalah*, it is the formula of consecration pronounced before every sacred recitation and every ritual act. According to another tradition, generally held to go back to the Caliph 'Alī, the cousin and son-in-law of the Prophet, the *basmalah* is in essence contained in its first letter, *ba*, and this again in its diacritical point, which thus symbolizes principial Unity.

In the conventional translation of the *basmalah* quoted above, the interpretation of the two names *ar-Raḥmān* and *ar-Raḥīm* as "the Compassionate" and "the Merciful" is only approximate as there is no real equivalent. Both names imply the idea of Mercy (*ar-Raḥmah*: *ar-Raḥmān* corresponds to the Mercy which—to use a Qur'ānic expression—"embraces all things", and expresses the plenitude of Being, Its essential bliss, and the universal nature of Its effulgence; *ar-Raḥīm* corresponds to Grace. As *Raḥmān* God manifests Himself through the appearance of the world; as *Raḥīm* He manifests Himself divinely within the world.)

[9] St. Denis the Areopagite writes in the same sense: ". . . If, therefore, in things divine, affirmation is less right and negation more true, it is expedient that we should not seek to set out, in forms analogous to them, those secrets that are wrapped in a holy obscurity for by no means does it abase but rather elevate the celestial beauties to depict them by means which are evidently inexact, since by that we avow that there is a whole world between them and material objects. . . . Further we must remember that nothing of what exists is wholly deprived of a certain beauty: for, as the Truth itself says, all things that were made are essentially good" (*Of the Celestial Hierarchy*). If a symbol and its archetype are incommensurable, there is none the less, as St. Denis explains in another passage, a strict analogy between the former and the latter.

The three Divine Names mentioned in the *basmalah* reflect one might say three "phases" or "dimensions" of the Divine Infinity. The name *Allāh* symbolizes, through its indeterminate character, the Infinite in its absolute transcendence: through His infinity God is "rich in Himself". The name *ar-Raḥmān* expresses "superabundant Infinity" by the very fact that the Infinite does not exclude any possible reality whatever, even Its own apparent limitation; It is the cause of the world; the manifestation of the world is a pure "mercy", for by it God opens Himself out to possibilities of limitation which neither add anything to His Essential Plenitude nor in any way limit it.

The name *ar-Raḥīm* expresses "Immanent Infinity": the world, which seems to limit the Infinite, in reality only limits itself; it could not exclude the Infinite, which descends mysteriously into it and, virtually, reabsorbs it into Its Plenitude. The Divine Infinity necessarily includes this triad of aspects.

The following is a translation of the *sūrat* (*al-Fātiḥah*), which "opens" the Qur'ān:

> Praise to God, the Lord of the worlds,
> The Compassionate, the Merciful,
> The King of the day of Judgment.
> It is Thee whom we adore and it is with Thee we seek refuge.
> Lead us on the straight way,
> The way of those on whom is Thy grace,
> Not (that of) those who suffer Thy wrath, nor of those who stray.

The tripartite division is traditional. The first part, as far as the words "The King of the day of Judgment", mentions the chief aspects of the Divinity; the last part, beginning with the words: "Lead us on the straight way", enumerates the fundamental tendencies of man; the verse between these expresses the relation between God and man, which has two aspects: dependence and participation.

By praise (*al-ḥamd*) offered to God the spirit soars, mind takes wing; its starting point may be any earthly object which does not amount to a mere limitation, anything which is not merely a "fact" and nothing more; every positive quality includes a depth of inexhaustible reality; every color, for instance, is both evident and unfathomable in its essential uniqueness, a uniqueness which reveals the Unique Being, "Lord of the worlds".

Being Itself is effaced before the Infinite and the Infinite is manifested by Being through the two "dimensions" described above, the "static" plenitude of *ar-Raḥmān* and the "dynamically" redemptive and immanent plenitude of *ar-Raḥīm*. Or again, the Bliss-and-Mercy (*ar-Raḥmah*) opens up and completes the creature, whereas Rigor (*al-Jalāl*) which is an expression of the Divine "Majesty" or Transcendence, constricts the creature and makes him powerless.

In the order of the categories of individual existence it is time which manifests the Divine Rigor. Consuming this world and all the beings in it, it recalls to them their "debt" to the Principle of their existence. The totality of time, its full cycle is "the day (for payment) of the debt" (*yawm-ad-dīn*), the words equally signifying "the day of religion", for religion is like the recognition of a debt.[10] The same expression also means "the day of judgment", which is nothing other than the final reintegration of the cycle of time into the timeless. This reintegration can be conceived on different scales according to whether we envisage the end of a man, the end of this world, or the end of the whole manifested universe—for "all things perish save His Face" as the Qur'ān says.

In the timeless the freedom which is but loaned to individual beings returns to its Divine Source; on "that day" God alone is "absolute King": the very essence of "free-will", its unconditioned basis, is thenceforth identified with the Divine Act. In God alone do freedom, action, and truth coincide,[11] and that is why some Sufis say that at the

[10] "Debt" is also one of the meanings of the Latin word *religio.*

[11] Freedom being everywhere what it is, that is, without inner constraint, it may be said that man is free to damn himself, just as he is free to throw himself, if he wishes, into an abyss; but as soon as man passes to action freedom becomes illusory in so far as it goes against truth: to cast oneself voluntarily into an abyss is to deprive oneself by the same act of freedom to act. It is the same for a man of infernal tendency: he becomes the slave of his choice, whereas the man of spiritual tendency rises towards a greater freedom. Again, since the reality of hell is made of illusion—the remoteness from God can only be illusory—hell cannot exist eternally beside Bliss, although it is unable to conceive its own end, this inability being, as it were, the counterfeit of Eternity in the states of damnation. Thus it is not without reason that Sufis have insisted on the relativity of everything created and have affirmed that after an indefinite duration the fires of hell will grow cold; all beings will finally be reabsorbed into God. Whatever modern philosophers may think, there is a contradiction between freedom and the arbitrary;

Last Judgment beings will judge themselves in God; this agrees with the Qur'ānic text which says it is man's members which accuse him.

Man is judged according to his essential tendency; this may be in conformity with the Divine attraction, or opposed to it, or it may be in a state of indecision between the two directions, and these are respectively the ways of "those on whom is Thy grace", of "those who suffer Thy wrath", and of "those who stray", who are dispersed in the indefinitude of existence and may be said to be turning round and round. In speaking of these three tendencies the Prophet drew a cross: the "straight way" is the ascending vertical; the "Divine wrath" acts in the opposite direction, and the dispersion of "those who stray" is in the horizontal direction.

These same fundamental tendencies are to be found in the whole universe; they constitute the ontological dimensions of "height" (*aṭ-ṭūl*), "depth" (*al-'umq*), and "breadth" (*al-'urḍ*). Hinduism calls these three cosmic tendencies (*guṇas*) *sattva*, *rajas*, and *tamas*, *sattva* expressing conformity to the Principle, *rajas* centrifugal dispersion, and *tamas* the fall, not only in a dynamic and cyclical sense, of course, but also in a static and existential sense.[12]

It can equally be said that for man there is only one essential tendency, that which brings him back to his own eternal Essence; all the other tendencies are merely the expression of creaturely ignorance and will moreover be cut off and judged. Asking God to lead us on the straight way is thus nothing but aspiration towards our own pre-temporal Essence. According to the Sufi exegesis the "straight way" (*aṣ-ṣirāṭ al-mustaqīm*) is the unique Essence of beings, as is indicated by this verse of the *Surat Hūd*: "There is no living creature which He (God) does not hold by its forelock;[13] verily my Lord is on a straight path" (11:56). Thus this prayer corresponds to the essential and fundamental request of every creature; it is granted by the mere fact of its utterance.

man is free to choose what is absurd, but inasmuch as he chooses it he is not free. In the creature freedom and action do not coincide.

[12] If stupidity, error, vice, ugliness, etc., are manifestations of *tamas*, the same is true, on another scale, of matter, weight, darkness, etc., but these categories are then "neutral" and so susceptible to a positive as well as a negative symbolism.

[13] This recalls the Hindu symbolism in which a being is linked to the Principle by the medium of the "solar ray" (*suṣumnā*) passing through the crown of the head.

Man's aspiration towards God includes the two aspects expressed in the verse: "It is Thee whom we adore (or serve) and it is with Thee we seek refuge (or help)." Adoration is the effacing of individual will before the Divine Will which is revealed externally by the sacred Law and inwardly by the movements of Grace. Recourse to Divine help is a participating in the Divine Reality through Grace and, more directly, through Knowledge. Ultimately the words: "It is Thee whom we adore" correspond to "extinction" (*al-fanā'*) and the words: "with Thee we seek refuge" to "subsistence" (*al-baqā'*) in Pure Being. Thus the verse just mentioned is the "isthmus" or *barzakh* between the two "oceans" of absolute Being and relative existence.[14]

[14] Cf. the Qur'ānic verses: "(God) produced the two seas which meet; between the two is an isthmus which they do not pass" (55:19-20).

PART TWO

THE DOCTRINAL FOUNDATIONS

Chapter 7

THE ASPECTS OF UNITY

The Islamic doctrine is contained as a whole in the *Tawḥīd*, the "affirmation of the Divine Unity". For the ordinary believer this affirmation is the clear and simple axis of the religion. For the contemplative it is the door which opens on to essential reality. The further the mind of the contemplative penetrates into the apparent rational simplicity of the Divine Unity, the more complex that simplicity will become; till a point is reached where its different aspects can no longer be reconciled by discursive thought alone. Meditation on these contrasts will in fact take the faculty of thought to its very furthest limits and the intelligence will in this way be opened to a synthesis lying beyond all formal conception. In other words it is only intuition beyond form that has access to Unity.

This applies to the fundamental formula of Islam, the "testimony" (*shahādah*) that "there is no divinity if it be not The Divinity" (*lā ilāha ill-Allāh*), which, so to say, "defines" the Divine Unity. This formula should be translated as here indicated and not, as usually the case, "there is no god but Allah", for it is proper to retain in it the appearance of pleonasm or paradox.

Its first part, "the negation" (*an-nafy*), denies in a general manner the same idea of divinity (*ilāh*) which the second part, the "affirmation" (*al-ithbāt*), affirms by isolation; in other words the formula as a whole postulates an idea—that of divinity—which at the same time it denies as a genus. This is the exact opposite of a "definition", for to define something means first to determine its "specific difference" and then to bring it to the "nearest genus", i.e. to general concepts. Now, as the *shahādah* indicates, Divinity is "defined" precisely by the fact that Its reality eludes every category. This paradox is analogous to that implied in the Taoist formulas: "The Way which can be followed is the (true) way" and "The Name which can be named is not the (true) name".[1] In this case, as in that of the Islamic "testimony", an idea is provisionally offered to thought and then withdrawn from all categories of thought.

[1] These are the first words of the *Tao Te Ching*.

The formula "There is no divinity if it be not The Divinity" contains simultaneously two meanings apparently in opposition one to the other: on the one hand it distinguishes between other-than-God and God Himself and, on the other hand, it brings the former back to the latter. Thus it expresses at the same time the most fundamental distinction and the identity of essence and is thus a résumé of the whole of metaphysic.

According to this "testimony" God is distinct from all things and nothing can be compared to Him, for between realities which can be compared one to another there is something in common in their nature or else an equality of condition, whereas the Divinity is transcendent in both respects. Now perfect incomparability requires that nothing can be set face to face with the incomparable and have any relationship whatever with it; this amounts to saying that nothing exists in face of the Divine Reality so that, in It, all things are annihilated. "God was and nothing with Him and He is now such as He was" (*ḥadīth qudsī*).[2]

Thus extreme "remoteness" (*tanzīh*) must imply its opposite. Since nothing can be opposed to God—for it would then be another "divinity" (*ilāh*)—every reality can only be a reflection of the Divine Reality. Moreover, every positive meaning one might give to the expression *ilāh* (divinity) will be transposed *in divinis*: "there is no reality if it be not The Reality", "there is no force if it be not The Force", "there is no truth if it is not The Truth". We must not seek to conceive God by bringing Him down to the level of things; on the contrary, things are reabsorbed into God so soon as one recognizes the essential qualities of which they are constituted. This is the point of view of symbolism (*tashbīh*) which is the complement of *tanzīh*.

Sufi masters call the indivisible Unity *al-Aḥadīyah*, a term derived from *aḥad*, which is the noun meaning "one", while to Unity as it appears in its universal aspects they give the name *al-Wāḥidīyah*, derived from *wāḥid*, the adjective meaning "unique". This term is here translated as "Uniqueness".

The supreme and incomparable Unity is without "aspects": it cannot be known at the same time as the world; that is, it is the object only of Divine, immediate, and undifferentiated Knowledge. Uniqueness (*al-Wāḥidīyah*), on the other hand, is in a sense a correlative of the Universe and it is in it that the Universe appears divinely.

[2] A saying of the Prophet that is divinely inspired.

In each of its aspects—and they are beyond number—God reveals Himself uniquely and all are integrated in the unique Divine Nature.[3] This distinction between the Divine Unity and the Divine Uniqueness is analogous to the Vedantic distinction between *Brahma nirguṇa* (Brahma unqualified) and *Brahma saguṇa* (Brahma qualified).

Logically, Unity is at the same time undifferentiated and the principle of all distinctions. As indivisible unity, in the sense of *al-Aḥadīyah,* it corresponds to what Hindus call "Non-Duality" (*advaita*)*;* as Uniqueness, in the sense of *al-Wāḥidīyah,* it is the positive content of every distinction, for it is by its intrinsic uniqueness that each being is distinct apart from the distinction by its mere limitations. Things are distinguished by their qualities and these, in so far as they are positive, can be transposed into the universal realm according to the formula: "There is no perfection if it be not The (Divine) Perfection." Now Universal Qualities are connected with the Divine Uniqueness for they are like possible "aspects" of the Divine Essence immanent in the world.

In regard to the Unique Being revealing Himself in them, they can be compared to rays emanating from the Principle from which they are never separate, and these rays light up all relative possibilities. They are in some way the "uncreated content" of created things, and it is through the medium of them that the Divinity is accessible, subject to the proviso that the Supreme Essence (*adh-Dhāt*),[4] in which their distinctive realities coincide, remains inaccessible from a relative starting-point. The outspreading of these rays is symbolized by the sun whose rays we see, though we cannot look on it itself directly because of its blinding brilliance.

We must not lose sight of the fact that the principial aspects of Being are also fundamental modalities of knowledge; the Universal Qualities are in the Intellect as they are also in the Essence; in both,

[3] Various triads can be conceived in the Divine Uniqueness and 3 is moreover the number which is the most immediate "image" of Unity. But none of the triads envisaged by Sufism is strictly analogous to the Christian Trinity, which is itself logically linked with the descent of the Eternal Word envisaged according to a perspective wherein consists the originality of Christianity.

[4] The term "Essence", here taken as the equivalent of the Arabic *adh-Dhāt*, is used both in the sense of the active pole of Universal Existence, as when the cosmic "essence" and "substance" are spoken of, and in the sense of the Absolute and Infinite Reality, when It is "opposed", through Its transcendence, to Being and so, *a fortiori*, to the Universe.

they can be compared to the different colors included in white light. The whiteness of the light is moreover really an absence of color, and this is analogous to the fact that the Essence, which synthesizes all the Qualities (*Ṣifāt*), cannot be known on the same plane as the Qualities.

For the mind the perfect Qualities are abstract ideas; for intuition, which "tastes" the essence of things, they are more real than are things themselves. All that Sufis teach about the Divine Qualities the contemplatives of the Eastern Orthodox Church say of the Divine "Energies", which they equally consider as uncreated but immanent in the world: the "Energies" cannot be detached from the Essence (Greek: *Ousia*) which they manifest and yet are distinct from it. This is something which, as St. Gregory Palamas puts it, can be conceived only through an intuition which "distinguishes the Divine Nature by uniting it, and unites it by distinguishing it".

This same truth is expressed in the Sufi formula which defines the relation of the Qualities to God: "neither He nor other than He" (*lā huwa wa lā ghayruhu*). The Essence, says St. Gregory Palamas, is "incommunicable, indivisible, and ineffable and is beyond every name and all understanding"; It is never manifested "outside Its own Ipseity", but Its very Nature implies "a supra-temporal act" of revelation by virtue of which It becomes in a certain manner accessible to creatures in the sense that "the creature is united with the Divinity in Its Energies".[5]

The Divine Qualities, each of which is unique, are indefinite in number. As for the Divine Names, they are necessarily limited in number, being nothing other than the Qualities summarized in certain fundamental types and "promulgated" by Sacred Scriptures as "means of grace" which can be "invoked". But Sufis speak of "Divine Names" meaning by that all the universal possibilities or essences included in the Divine Essence immanent in the world. This terminology is only an extension of the symbolism of the Qur'ān. In the Qur'ān God reveals Himself by His Names, just as He manifests Himself in the universe through His perfect Qualities.[6]

[5] See *The Ascetic and Theological Doctrine of St. Gregory Palamas* by the monk Wassily Krivochene of the monastery of St. Pantaleimon on Mount Athos, translated into German by Fr. H. Landvogt (Wurzburg, 1939).

[6] In Sufi language the Divine Names designate, as supports for invocation, both what Christian scholasticism calls "the Presence of Immensity", which particularly corre-

When considered as a determination, the Names or Qualities are "universal relationships" (*nisab kullīyah*), "non-existent" in themselves and so "virtual" and permanent in the Essence. They are only manifested, i.e. known in a distinctive mode, in so far as their implicit terms, such as active and passive, are defined. This amounts to saying that the Divine Names or Qualities "exist" only so much as the world "exists". From another angle we may say that all the Qualities of the world are logically reducible to the universal Qualities, or in other words to pure relationships.[7]

sponds to the Qualities, and "the Indwelling Presence". The former relates to the universal immanence of God in the world and the latter to His "Real Presence" in the sacraments and in contemplative vision. On the Sufi theory of Divine Presence (*Ḥadarāt*) see the chapter on Union of this book.

[7] Some Sufi masters envisage a Divine aspect intermediate between Unity and Uniqueness which they call the Divine Solitude (*Waḥdah*). In this the possibilities of distinction or manifestation are principially "conceived" without being actually deployed. Divine Solitude includes in Itself four principial "faces": Knowledge (*al-ʿIlm*), Consciousness (*ash-Shuhūd*), Light (*an-Nūr*), and Being (*al-Wujūd*). The idea of "consciousness" must here be transposed beyond its psychological aspect: it is the quality of witness (*shahīd*).

Chapter 8

CREATION

"Behold what shows to thee His Omnipotence, (may He be exalted): it is that He hides Himself from thee by what has no existence apart from Him."

(Ibn ʿAṭāʾillāh al-Iskandarī, in his *Ḥikam*)

The idea of creation, which is common to the three monotheistic[1] religions, in appearance contradicts the idea of the essential Unity of all beings, since *creatio ex nihilo* seems to deny the pre-existence of possibilities in the Divine Essence and in consequence to deny also their subsistence in It, whereas the idea of manifestation as taught in Hinduism relates relative beings to Absolute Essence as reflections are related to their luminous source.

However, these two conceptions or symbolisms approach one another if we consider that the metaphysical meaning of the "nothingness" (*ʿudum*) whence the Creator "draws" things can only be the "nothingness" of "non-existence", i.e. of non-manifestation or the principial state, since the possibilities principially contained in the Divine Essence are not distinct in It as such before they are deployed in a relative mode. They are also not "existing" (*mawjūd*) for existence already implies a first condition and a virtual distinction of "knower" from "known". As for the action of "creating" in the sense of the Arabic word *khalaqa*, it is synonymous with "assigning to each thing its proper measure". This, transposed into the metaphysical order, corresponds to the first determination (*taʿayyun*) of possibilities in the Divine Intellect. According to this meaning of the word *khalq*, "creation" can be envisaged as logically preceding the "production to existence" (*ījād*) of these same possibilities.

Thus cosmogony can be described in this way: first God "conceives" the possibilities susceptible of manifestation in a state of perfect simultaneity and assigns to each its "capacity" (*qadr*) to develop

[1] The conventional term "monotheistic" is used here for want of a better for indeed every true tradition recognizes a single supreme principle.

in a relative mode; then He brings them into existence[2] by manifesting (*ẓahara*) Himself in them. Thus, in His quality of Creator (*Khāliq*), God operates a choice of the possibilities to manifest. And so it is that creation appears inasmuch as it is related to the Divine Person (*an-Nafs*) conceived by analogy with the human person and designated by attributes such as Judgment (*al-ḥukm*), Will (*al-iradāh*), and Action (*al-fiʿl*); now the anthropomorphism of these expressions is only an "allusion" (*ishārah*) and not a limitation of the perspective in question.

There is, however, a metaphysical perspective which is wider and considers things in relation to the Infinity of the Divine Essence. In the sight of the Infinite all possibilities are what they are eternally; in the Divine Knowledge all possibilities are contained such as they are with whatever each of them implies of permanent or relative actuality, and thus the choice of possibilities of manifestation coincides with their very nature; or, again, from an aspect which is the complement of this, the Divine Being manifests Himself according to all possible modes,[3] and there is no limit to the Divine possibilities.

From all these different points of view the world is essentially the manifestation of God to Himself. Thus it is expressed in the sacred saying (*ḥadīth qudsī*)[4] which brings back the idea of creation to the idea of Knowledge: "I was a hidden treasure; I wished to be known (or, to know) and I created the world." In the same sense Sufis compare the Universe to a combination of mirrors in which the Infinite Essence contemplates Itself in a multiplicity of forms, or which reflect in differing degrees the irradiation (*at-tajallī*) of the One Being. These mirrors symbolize the possibilities of the Essence (*adh-Dhāt*) to deter-

[2] Moreover, the Divine Name of Creator (*al-Khāliq*) is deemed to be hierarchically superior to that of Producer (*al-Bāri*) as this in turn is superior to the Name of He-Who-Gives-form (*al-Muṣawwir*), and this is the order in which these three Names are enumerated in the Qurʾān (59:24), for form is secondary in relation to existence. This also shows that the first "determination" of possibilities, according to the metaphysical meaning of the word *Khāliq*, is beyond form.

[3] In conformity with this every "theory of knowledge" comes to two complementary "definitions", both equally valid: either things appear in a unique knowledge, principially present in every being, or every individual being "subjectivizes" after its own fashion a unique and universal Being. Without uniqueness in principle, there is no knowledge at all. In his *Futūḥāt al-Makkiyah* Ibn ʿArabī writes that the principial possibilities (*al-aʿyūn*) are reflected in the Divine Being (*al-Wujūd*), or that the Divine Being is reflected in the principial possibilities, according to the point of view adopted.

[4] A saying of the Prophet that is divinely inspired.

mine Itself, possibilities which It contains by virtue of Its Infinity (*Kamāl*).

Such at least is the purely principial meaning of the mirrors, but they also have a cosmological meaning, that of receptive substances (*qawābil*) passive in relation to the pure Act (*al-Amr*). In either case we have a polarity, but it is integrated in Unity, for of the two opposing terms, the higher is resolved in the Divine Being (*al-Wujūd*) which is nothing other than the first affirmation, perfect and unconditioned, of the Essence (*adh-Dhāt*),[5] whereas the lower finds its resolution in the "principial possibilities" (*al-aʿyān ath-thābitah*), and these are themselves likewise reducible to the Essence, of which they are merely "determinations" or "relations" (*nisab*), "non-existent as such, though permanent" (Ibn ʿArabī, in the chapter on Enoch, of his *Fuṣūṣ al-Ḥikam*).

It must be clearly understood that this purely logical opposing of Being and "principial possibilities" does not at all envisage distinct cosmic entities but in a sense represents a speculative key to the reintegration of all possible qualities in the Unity of the Essence, though it also corresponds to a precise metaphysical reality. As for the symbolism connected with it which presents Divine Being as a source of light, the "out-pouring" or "overflowing" (*al-fayḍ*) of which spreads out on to the possibilities, which can themselves be compared to a dark space,[6] this must not be understood in the sense of a substantial emanation, for it is clear that Being could not go outside Itself, since nothing is outside It.

Being reveals the Essence by affirmation whereas the principial possibilities are reducible to It by a sort of negation since they are only limitations, at any rate to the extent that we can separate them logically from Being. "In truth", writes Ibn ʿArabī in his *Fuṣūṣ al-Ḥikam*, "all possibilities (*mumkināt*) are principially reducible to non-existence (*ʿudum*) and there is no Being (or, Existence) other than the Being of God, may He be exalted, (revealing Himself) in the 'forms' of the states which result from possibilities as they are in themselves in their essential determinations" (in the chapter on Jacob).

This distinction of Being from the principial possibilities or immutable essences—a distinction which is at the very limit of what

[5] In itself the Essence is apart from every determination—even from that of Being (*Wujūd*). It is at the same time Being and Non-Being (*Wujūd wa ʿUdum*).

[6] Light and Space are the two most direct symbols of Being and of Possibility.

is conceivable and is resolved in the Divine Infinity—allows us to envisage universal manifestation in two complementary relationships, on the one hand in that of "auto-determinations" or "subjectivations" (*ta'ayyunāt*) of the Essence, and on the other in that of the divine "revelations" (*tajallīyāt*) which appear in them. Being is conceived by integration, so that it reaffirms Itself as one in each manifested possibility and as alone in all, whereas the possibilities as such establish diversity without ever being essentially detached from the One.

If the metaphysical distinction thus established is indisputable and if it can be defined by logical formulae, it is none the less true that it does not pertain to the rational level. The coincidence of Being (*Wujūd*) and the principial possibilities (*a'yān*)—which, according to Ibn 'Arabī, have "never so much as sensed the odor of existence"—is as paradoxical as the coincidence of "existence" (*Wujūd*) and "absence" (*'udum*), and it is precisely in this that is expressed both the "voidness" of things—to use the Buddhist expression—and their character of pure symbols.

Chapter 9

THE ARCHETYPES

The "Principial Possibilities" or "immutable essences" (*al-aʿyān ath-thābitah*), though they are contained in the Divine Essence where there is no distinction, are also, in so far as they are reflected in the universal Intellect, the "Ideas" or archetypes which Plato compares, in his parable of the cave, to real objects of which the prisoners in the cave perceive only the shadows.

In this sense—inasmuch, that is, as Sufis adopt the theory of archetypes—they are all necessarily "Platonists". The doctrine of archetypes is, moreover, integrally connected with that of Divine Omniscience. This is shown by the Persian Sufi Nūr ad-Dīn ʿAbd ar-Raḥmān Jāmī in his treatise *Lawāʾih*:[1] ". . . The true essence of everything always abides, though unmanifest in the inner depths of very Being, while its sensory qualities appear outwardly. For it is impossible that the Divine 'Ideas' included in the intelligible world should be evanescent: (to pretend that the content of Divine Science is evanescent) would imply atheism. . ." (chapter 22).

The arguments adduced by certain philosophers against the existence of the Platonic "Ideas" fall completely to the ground if it is understood that these "Ideas" have no *existence*, as Ibn ʿArabī puts it, or in other words that they are not of the nature of distinct substances and constitute only possibilities inherent in the Intellect and principially inherent in the Divine Essence. Further, the whole of the philosophical discussions on "universals" proceed from a confusion between archetypes and their reflections on a purely mental level. It is clear that, as mental forms, general ideas are only pure abstractions, but to establish this does not touch the Platonic archetypes or "Ideas", since these are only intellectual dispositions or possibilities, possibili-

[1] English translation by E.H. Whinfield and Mirza Muhammad Kazvini in Oriental Translation Fund, N.S., Vol. XVI. In large part this treatise is a commentary on the *Fuṣūṣ al-Ḥikam* of Ibn ʿArabī and it can be considered as a summary of Sufi metaphysic. In the English translation *ʿayn* (plural, *aʿyān*) is sometimes translated as "substance". Since this can lead to great confusion the word is here translated as "essence" or as "principial possibility". *ʿAyn* can also mean "eye", "spring", and individual essence.

ties presupposed by the "abstractions" which, without them, would be wholly lacking in intrinsic truth.

To deny the "immutable essence", the source of all relative knowledge, would be like denying space on the pretext that it has no spatial form. In fact the archetypes are never manifested as such either in the sensory or in the mental field. None the less everything within those fields comes back, principially, to them. If we seek to grasp them they elude distinctive vision; they can be known only intuitively, either through their symbols or by identification with the Divine Essence.

Here let it be noted that the expression *dhikr* in the Qur'ān means "memory" in the Platonic sense of reflected knowledge of the archetypes, with this shade of difference that the word *dhikr* means literally "mention". Thus the Qur'ānic phrase *fadhkurūnī adhkurkum* (2:152) can be translated either as "Remember Me and I will remember you" or as "Mention Me and I will mention you". Now it is by an inner "mention" that a memory is evoked: moreover the transposition of the past to the principial order conforms to the general symbolism of Semitic languages: in Arabic the past definite tense serves to express the timeless action of God. This double aspect of the word *dhikr* plays an important part in the language of Sufism, for it connects the "evoking" of essential Realities with the sonorous symbolism of the formulas of "incantation" or "invocation" (*dhikr*).[2] Moreover, *dhikr* is the word used to designate every form of concentration on the Divine Presence: the highest "remembrance" or "mention" is no less than identification with the Divine Word which is itself the Archetype of archetypes.

The reader will have gathered that the "remembrance" of Sufism, like the Platonic "reminiscence", is not psychological but intellectual. It is precisely because of this that it can take for its supports things of an elemental order and, in particular, bodily form. Nothing is more false than to look on methods of incantation as a more "primary" and so less "conscious" form of adoration than, for example, free prayer. There is a link of inverse analogy between the most elemental cosmic order and the most lofty spiritual order and it is on this account that the supports which help to transform consciousness into the Spirit, which is beyond form, are allied to the great rhythms of nature, the movements of the stars, the waves of the sea, or the spasms of love and of dying.

[2] Analogous to the *mantra-yoga* (*japa*) of the Hindus.

Chapter 10

THE "RENEWING OF CREATION AT EACH INSTANT"

There is an aspect of the Sufi theory of Creation called the "Renewing of Creation at each instant", or, "at each breath" (*Tajdīd al-khalq bil'-anfās*), and it is very directly connected with spiritual realization. It was said above that the "immutable essence" (*al-a'yān ath-thābitah*), the pure possibilities in which God manifests Himself to Himself, are never, as such, brought forth to existence and that only their relative modalities—all the possible relations (*nisab*) they imply—are deployed in the Universe. Nor do these latter really "come out" from their archetypes, and their variety is never exhausted in a mode of succession, even as the waves of a river never cease from changing their form while at the same time obeying the law imposed on them by the configuration of the river-bed.

In this picture, imperfect just because it is concrete, the river water represents the incessant "outpouring" or "flux" (*fayd*) of Being and the river-bed "immutable determination" while the waves correspond to form, either sensory or subtle, resulting from this ontological polarity. The "immutable essence", or the archetype, can also be compared to a colorless prism which breaks up the light of Being into rays of all the colors of the rainbow, the coloring of the rays depending both on the essential nature of the light and on the nature of the prism.

In the world which is beyond form or the spiritual world (*'ālam al-arwāḥ*, or *al-Jabarūt*) the variety of the reflections of one single archetype appears as a "richness" of its aspects, one contained within another as are the many logical aspects of one single truth or the beatitudes included in a single beauty. At this level of existence their variety is as far as possible from any repetition because it directly expresses the Divine Uniqueness. At the same time, the different archetypes mutually include one another. In the world of individuation, on the other hand, the reflections of an archetype manifest themselves successively because here the cosmic condition of form enters in as a delimitation or reciprocal exclusion of the various aspects.

It is this world—and it includes psychic as well as bodily forms—which is called the "world of analogies" or the "world of the alike" (*'ālam al-mithāl*)[1] because the forms which in it are manifested successively or simultaneously are analogous one to another through being analogous to their common archetype. In the lower levels of existence, such as the corporeal world (*'ālam al-ajsām*)—the variety of forms closely approaches repetition, expressed by the quantitative mode, but never reaches it, for in pure repetition all the distinct qualities which constitute the world would be dissolved.

If the variety of the reflections of one single archetype is envisaged in connection with their temporal succession, which may be taken as a symbolical expression of all possible succession, then it is said that the "projection" of the archetype into existence is renewed at each instant in such a way that the same state of "reflected" existence never subsists. Thus a relative being is subject to continual annihilation and continual renewal. In his *Fuṣūṣ al-Ḥikam* Muḥyi-d-Dīn ibn 'Arabī writes that "man does not spontaneously arrive at a clear idea of the fact that at each 'breath' he is not and then again is (*lam yakun thumma kāna*). And, if I say, 'then', I am not supposing any temporal interval but only a purely logical succession. In 'the Renewing of Creation at each breath' the instant of annihilation coincides with the instant of the manifestation of its like (*mathal*)" (from the chapter on Solomon).

In the same sense 'Abd ar-Razzāq al-Qāshānī[2] writes in his commentary on *The Wisdom of the Prophets* that "there is no temporal interval between annihilation and re-manifestation, so that we do not perceive any interruption between two analogous and successive creations, and thus existence appears to us to be homogeneous". According to Muḥyi-d-Dīn ibn 'Arabī this illusion of continuity is "expressed by the saying in the Qur'ān that 'they are deceived by a new creation'[3] which means that for them not an instant passes without their perceiving what they perceive. . ." (*The Wisdom of the Prophets*). This recalls the Buddhist parable which compares existence to the flame of an oil lamp; this flame, though it seems the same, never ceases to be renewed at each instant, so that in reality it is neither the same nor yet another.

[1] This is also called the "world of imagination" (*'ālam al-khayāl*).

[2] A thirteenth-century Sufi master who wrote a commentary on the *Fuṣūṣ al-Ḥikam* of Ibn 'Arabī.

[3] "Are We exhausted by the first creation? Assuredly they are deceived by a new creation" (50:15).

In order to complete this Buddhist picture from the Sufi point of view[4] it must be added that the flame as such corresponds to Being (*al-Wujūd*) whereas the form of the flame reflects the archetype, and that it is to the archetype that the flame owes its relative continuity. If it is true that the flame has no autonomous existence, it is equally true that it exists. Thus there is in the cosmos an "absolute" discontinuity which expresses its illusory character and brings us back to the fundamental discontinuity between the world and God.

On the other hand there is also in the cosmos an "absolute" continuity inasmuch as it is wholly a reflection of its Divine Cause. ʿAbd ar-Razzāq al-Qāshānī wrote further of this that "in so far as man is a possibility of manifestation, but does not see Him Who manifests him, he is pure absence (*ʿudum*): but on the other hand in so far as he receives his being from the perpetual irradiation (*Tajallī*) of the Essence, he *is*. The ceaseless revelation of the Divine Activities which flows from the Divine Names renews him after each annihilation, and that instantaneously without any perceptible temporal succession but following a purely logical succession. For here there is only one permanent non-existence—that of pure possibility—and only one permanent Being—the revelation of the one Essence—and then there are activities and individuations succeeding one another with the 'breaths' which proceed from the Divine Names. . ." (commentary on *The Wisdom of the Prophets*).

As for the "breaths" or "exhalations" (*anfās*) referred to in this text, they are modalities of the "Exhalation of the Merciful" (*Nafas ar-Raḥmān* or *an-Nafas ar-Raḥmānī*), this term being understood in the sense of the divine principle which "dilates" (*nafassa*)[5] or deploys relative possibilities starting from the archetypes. This "dilation" only appears as such from a relative point of view in which the state of "inwardness" (*buṭūn*) of the possibilities appears as a "contraction" (*karb*). The Divine "Exhalation" is connected with the total Mercy (*ar-Raḥmah*) because it is through this Mercy that the superabundance of Being "overflows" (*afāḍa*) into limitless essences.

[4] In conformity with its own outlook, Buddhism but underlines the impermanence of the cosmos: for it the immutable Reality is identified with the "Void" (*Śūnya*) which cannot he expressed in positive terms. In an analogous sense Ibn ʿArabī speaks of the "non-existence" (*ʿudum*) of the archetypes.

[5] The same verb also includes the meaning of "consolation", in contrast to the "constriction" (*karb*) induced by distress. "Consolation" clearly comes from the Divine Mercy (*Raḥmah*).

At the same time the idea of "exhalation" or "breath" relates to the symbolism of the Divine Word, for, just as the different sounds or "letters" (*ḥurūf*)[6] which make up the sayings of the revealed Book are analogous to the archetypes which are reflected in the cosmos, so the breath which is the support or "carrier" of articulated sounds is analogous to the Divine Principle which deploys and supports the possibilities of manifestation.[7] The Divine "Exhalation" is the "dynamic" and "feminine" complement of the Divine Command (*al-Amr*), the pure Act expressed by the word "Be" (*kun*)[8] and corresponds, in the symbolism mentioned above, in some sense to the emitting of simple sound. In his *Futūḥāt al-Makkiyah* Muḥyi-d-Dīn ibn ʿArabī identifies the Divine "Exhalation" with universal Nature (*aṭ-Tabīʿah*) and attributes to the latter a cosmogonic function analogous to what Hindus call the *Shakti* or "Productive Energy" of Divinity. The expression "the renewing of creation at each breath", or "by breaths", must be understood through this symbolism.

As for the close connection between the theory just set out and spiritual realization, we need only say that the human soul is part of the "world of the alike" which includes not only this world but also the formal paradises and the hells; the soul is thus constituted by reflections which succeed one another indefinitely and without pause so that it has no true continuity and the identity of the "I" is only a recollection of the "Self"[9] (*al-huwiyah*), the possibility of the being which subsists eternally in the Infinite Essence. That which "lights up" and knows the unceasing flight of the "alike"[10] and connects them with their archetype is clearly not the individual consciousness but pure and transcendent Intelligence.

[6] Since Arabic writing is strictly phonetic the "letters" also designate sounds.

[7] In this lies a foundation of the science of invocation.

[8] According to the teaching of the Greek Fathers of the Christian Church the world was created "by the Son in the Holy Spirit". The Divine Command corresponds to the Word and so to the Son. It will be remembered that the Holy Spirit is also called "the Comforter", a term analogous to the Arabic verb *nafassa*. This analogy between the "Exhalation of the Merciful" and the Holy Spirit is valid only as regards the "economic" role of the Holy Spirit and not as regards the hypostatical person.

[9] The word *huwiyah* means, literally, "ipseity" and is derived from the pronoun *huwa*, "he", inasmuch as this is outside the opposition between "I" and "thou".

[10] This expression is from the Qurʾān: ". . . it is not We who will be forestalled from changing your 'likeness' (*amthālakum*) and from reproducing you under a form you know not" (56:60-61).

Chapter 11

THE SPIRIT

The universal Spirit (*ar-Rūḥ*), which is also called the "first Intellect" (*al-ʿAql al-awwal*), is described sometimes as created, sometimes as uncreated. According to the saying of the Prophet, "the first thing which God created is the Spirit (*ar-Rūḥ*)"; it is created, and, according to the passage in the Qurʾān where God says of Adam: "And I breathed into Him My Spirit", it is uncreated, because directly united with the Divine Nature. As for the verse in the Qurʾān which describes the nature of the Spirit in these words: "They will question you about the Spirit; say to them: The Spirit (proceeds) from the Command (*al-Amr*) of my Lord. . ." (17:85), this can be interpreted in either sense—that the Spirit is of the same nature as the Divine Command—or Order—which is of necessity uncreated since it is It which creates all things, or that the Spirit *proceeds* from the Order and is itself at an ontological level immediately below that Order.

If there are both these aspects of the Spirit it is because it is the mediator between the Divine Being and the conditioned universe. Uncreated in its immutable essence it is yet created inasmuch as it is the first Cosmic entity. It is compared to the supreme Pen (*al Qalam al-aʿlā*) with which God inscribes all destinies on the guarded Tablet (*al-Lawḥ al-Maḥfūz*) which itself corresponds to the universal Soul (*an-Nafs al-kulliyah*).[1] For the Prophet said that the "first thing God created is the Pen; He created the (guarded) Tablet and said to the Pen: Write! And the Pen replied: and what shall I write? (God) said to it: Write My Knowledge of My creation till the day of resurrection; then

[1] The individual soul is conditioned by form; the universal Soul is necessarily beyond form. In either case soul is to Spirit as is substance to essence, or *materia* to *forma*, this last expression being taken, not as form which limits but as the "formative" essence. Thus individuals are distinguished by virtue of the Spirit, just as they are essentially united in it, and are substantially united in the universal Soul while differentiated by virtue of their forms, the "plastic" support of which is precisely the universal or "total" Soul. In so far as the Spirit is polarized in a certain sense in relation to each particular being we can speak of many "spirits". The essential oneness of the Spirit thus in no wise implies that man's spirit is definitely reintegrated into It merely by the death of the body; for it is the soul which individualizes the spirit, and the soul is immortal.

the Pen traced what had been ordained." So the Spirit includes all the Divine Knowledge concerning created beings, and this means that it is the Truth of truths or the Reality of realities (*Ḥaqīqat al-Ḥaqā'iq*) or—according to the aspect in which it is envisaged—the direct and immediate manifestation of this Reality of realities.

Certain Sufi writers, such as 'Abd al-Karīm al-Jīlī, give the name Holy Spirit (*Rūḥ al-Quddūs*) to the uncreated essence of the Spirit and compare it to the Face of God (*Wajh Allāh*); this is what is here to be understood by the divine Intellect.

The uncreated essence of the Spirit corresponds to what Hindus call *Puruṣa* or *Puruṣottama*; its created nature corresponds to what they call *Buddhi*, the "Intellectual Light". Now *Buddhi* is the first product of *Prakṛti*, the universal "plastic" Substance,[2] and this amounts to saying that *Buddhi*, though supra-individual in its nature, is "created", for every "creature" participates in the passivity of Substance.

The Sufi term for universal Substance or the *Materia Prima* is *al-Ḥabā*. This designation of it goes back to the Caliph 'Alī the Prophet's spiritual successor, and signifies literally the "fine dust" suspended in the air which becomes visible only by the rays of light it refracts. The symbolism of *al-Ḥabā* illustrates the double nature of the Spirit, for it is the Spirit which illumines *al-Ḥabā* and thus corresponds to the ray of light refracted by fine dust. Since the dust becomes visible only to the extent that it refracts light, the ray only shows as such on the screen of the dust.

Undifferentiated light symbolizes the uncreated Spirit while the light determined as a ray on the other hand symbolizes the created Spirit, which is in a sense "directed" like a ray. As for the fine dust which is the symbol of *al-Ḥabā* this is a principle of differentiation which is invisible as such. This means—and it conforms to the symbolism of the light—that Substance has no true existence and can he grasped only through its effects. The most "gross" of its effects is precisely manifestation in quantitative mode, the picture of which is given as clearly as possible by the multitude of the dust particles. As for the dust lit up by the ray of light it is nothing other than the world.

[2] Substance—or the *Materia Prima*—also has the name *Hayūlā* derived from the Greek word *Hyle*.

Al-Ḥabā is to the uncreated Intellect as the universal Soul (*an-Nafs al-kullīyah*)[3] is to the created Intellect.[4] On the other hand the uncreated pair is in a sense the equivalent of universal Nature (*aṭ-Ṭabīʿah*) and the Divine Command (*al-Amr*), since universal Nature, itself principially identified with the Divine "Exhalation" (*an-Nafas ar-Raḥmānī*), is as the "maternal" aspect of substance (*al-Ḥabā*). Thus we have, theoretically, three cosmogonic pairs the terms of which are related to one another as masculine and feminine principles. But from the cosmological point of view it is only implicitly that the Spirit or Intellect is uncreated, for it is only the created Spirit which represents a reality distinct from God.

Again, the *Materia Prima* or Substance (*al-Ḥabā*) can be envisaged at different levels: as for its purely principial nature, which Ibn ʿArabī names the "Supreme Element" (*al-ʿUnṣur al-aʿẓam*), this is necessarily outside the scope of cosmology since it is only a non-manifested divine possibility. Such applications of the same terms to different degrees in the hierarchy of existence explain some of the seeming contradictions between one Sufi writer and another or even between different expositions by the same author.

As the mediator *par excellence* the Spirit is also the prototype of prophetic manifestations, and in this aspect is to be identified with the archangel Gabriel (*Jibrīl*) who announced the Word to the Virgin Mary and transmitted the Qurʾān to the Prophet.

The Divine Command (*al-Amr*).	Universal Nature (*aṭ-Ṭabīʿah*) or the Divine Exhalation (*Nafas ar-Raḥmānī*).
The Divine Intellect or the Holy Spirit (*Rūḥ al-Quddūs*).	The Supreme Element (*al-ʿUnṣur al-aʿẓam*) or principial Substance (*al-Ḥabā*).
The First Intellect (*al-ʿAql al-awwal*) or the Spirit (*ar-Rūḥ*) or the Supreme Pen (*al-Qalam al-aʿlā*).	Universal Soul (*an-Nafs al-kullīyah*) or the Guarded Tablet (*al-Lawḥ al Maḥfūz*).
The First Intellect or the Spirit.	*Materia Prima* or cosmic substance (*al-Ḥabā* or *al-Hayūlā*).

[3] The *Psyche* in Plotinus.

[4] The *Nous* in Plotinus.

The most "central" image of the Spirit on this earth is Man. But every form necessarily omits certain aspects of its prototype and so the Spirit reveals complementary and less "central" aspects of Itself in other terrestrial forms. For example it is revealed in the form of a tree of which the trunk symbolizes the axis of the Spirit passing through the whole hierarchy of worlds while its branches and leaves correspond to the differentiation of the Spirit in the many states of existence.

A Sufi legend, probably of Persian origin, tells that God created the Spirit in the form of a peacock and showed it in the mirror of the Divine Essence its own image. The peacock was seized with reverential dread (*al-haybah*) and let fall drops of sweat, and from these all other beings were created. The peacock's outspread tail imitates the cosmic deployment of the Spirit.

Another symbol of the Spirit is to be seen in the eagle which soars above the creatures of the earth, observes them from on high, and drops vertically on to its prey like a flash of lightning, for it is thus that intellectual intuition seizes its objects.

The white dove is also an image of the Spirit by reason of its color, its innocence, and the softness of its flight.

At the extreme limits of the sensory world the shining nature of the stars, and the transparence and incorruptibility of precious stones also recall aspects of the Universal Spirit.

Chapter 12

UNIVERSAL MAN

The Divine Act, which is one, has only one single object. From the Divine "point of view" creation is one and is summed up in a single prototype in which are reflected all the divine Qualities or "relationships" (*nisab*) without their being confused or separated. "In truth ... We have counted everything in a clear prototype (*imām*)" (Qur'ān, 36:12). From the point of view of the creation, on the other hand, the Universe can only be multiple since it is conceived as "other than-God" and God alone is one. Thus the unique prototype (*al-Unmūdhaj al-farīd*) is, from the relative point of view, differentiated into successive polarizations such as active and passive, macrocosm and microcosm, species and individual, man and woman,[1] each one of the elements of each of these opposed terms being endowed with its own perfection. The macrocosm, which manifests God inasmuch as He is "the Outer" (*aẓ-Ẓāhir*), is perfect because it includes all individual beings and thus expresses the divine stability and power: "Are ye then of a creation stronger than the heaven which He built. . ?" (Qur'ān, 79:27). The microcosm, which corresponds to the Divine Name "the Inner" (*al-Bāṭin*), is perfect by its central nature.

In the sight of the Essence, which is one, the universe is like a single being. The essential unity of the world is the most certain of things but also the most hidden: all knowledge and every perception, however adequate or inadequate, presupposes the essential Unity of beings and of things. If beings of different kinds perceive the universe differently according to differences in their perspective and in conformity with their level of universality, they none the less do perceive it really, for the reality of the universe cannot readily be dissociated from the reality of their vision and this reality is one although diverse

[1] These cosmic polarizations are often brought out at the beginning of *Sūrat*s of the Qur'ān, as in *Sūrat* 92:1-4: "By the night when it covers and by the day when it unveils and by that which created male and female! Verily your tendencies are divergent. . . ." Here night and day correspond to reabsorption in the unmanifest and to manifestation, male and female, to active and passive, and it is from these polarities that the divergent tendencies of men arise, tendencies such as the faith and unbelief, the generosity and the avarice mentioned in the rest of this *Sūrat*.

in its aspects; it is simultaneously present in the subjects who know and in the objects known. Again, duality and discontinuity are of the nature of the world; to see the world means not to see the Essence; to contemplate the Essence means not to see the world.

Among all the beings of this world man alone has a vision which in virtuality includes all things; other organic beings have only a partial vision of the world. Admittedly the direct and immediate content of human perception embraces only the surrounding corporeal world, but, on its own level of existence, this represents a relatively complete picture of the whole universe. Through sensory forms man conceives both subtle forms and spiritual essences. It may thus be said that man, who is a microcosm, and the universe, which is a macrocosm, are like two mirrors each reflecting the other. On the one hand man only exists in relation to the macrocosm which determines him, and on the other hand man knows the macrocosm, and this means that all the possibilities which are unfolded in the world are principially contained in man's intellectual essence. This is the meaning of the saying in the Qur᾽ān: "And He (God) taught Adam all the names (i.e. all the essences of beings and of things)" (2:31).

After its own fashion every microcosm is a center of the universe, but in man the "subjective" polarization of the Spirit reaches its culminating point: "He hath set in your service all that is in the heavens and on the earth—all comes from Him" (Qur᾽ān, 45:13). As for the non-human microcosm included in our world, these are inferior to man as microcosms, that is, they are inferior in so far as they are "subjective" polarizations of the Spirit or of the Unique Prototype, but they are relatively superior to man in so far as they participate more in the macrocosmic perfection. There is, down through the hierarchy of the animal and vegetable kingdoms, an increasing predominance of the species over individual autonomy[2] while in the case of minerals the two poles of species and individual are almost merged.

Each term of the successive polarizations of the unique Prototype contains, either implicitly or explicitly, its own complementary term. The species includes individuals, but each individual includes in itself a virtuality of all possibilities of the species. Man has in him the

[2] For this reason animals cannot sink in relation to their specific norm to the same extent as man; "Verily We have created man according to the most beautiful form; then We made him the vilest of the vile, save only those who believe and do good works. . ." (Qur᾽ān, 95:4-6).

nature of woman and vice versa and this is so from the very origin of beings. "Fear your Lord Who created you from a single soul (*min nafsin wāḥidah*), Who created from it its spouse and from this pair has produced men and women in great number" (Qur'ān, 4:1). In the same way the world or the macrocosm clearly "contains" man who is himself an integral part of it. But man knows the world and, given the principial unity of Being and Knowledge, this means that all the possibilities of the world are in a virtual and principial sense present in man. Man and the cosmos are, as was said above, like two mirrors each reflecting the other; hence the Sufi saying that "the universe is a big man and man a little universe" (*al-kawnu insānun kabīrun wa-l-insānu kawnun ṣaghīr*).

It may also be said that the universe and man are forms of the Universal Spirit (*ar-Rūḥ*) or of the Divine Spirit, or that the two are complementary aspects of one single "pancosmic" being, a symbol of God. However, the "outward" or "objective" form of the macrocosm cannot be grasped in its totality because its limits extend indefinitely, whereas the form of man is known. This leads us to say that man is a qualitative "abridgement" of the great cosmic "book", all universal qualities being in one way or another expressed in his form. Again, the Prophet said that "God created Adam in His (own) form", which means that the primordial nature of man is as it were the symbolical final term and in a sense the visible "sum" of all the divine essences immanent in the world.[3]

In the case of ordinary man the "global" meaning of human nature remains only a virtuality, and it is actualized only in one who has effectively realized all the universal Truths reflected in his terrestrial form and who is thus identified with the "Perfect Man" or with "Universal Man" (*al-Insān al-kāmil*). Practically speaking such a man will have his human individuality as his "external" form, but in their virtuality

[3] This was also the teaching of the Greek Fathers of the Christian Church and particularly of St. Gregory of Nyssa and St. Gregory Palamas. The latter wrote: "Man, this greater world in little compass, is an epitome of all that exists in a unity and is the crown of the Divine works. And moreover it was for this reason that he was created last, just as we in our final conclusions recapitulate our discourse; for one could also call the universe the work of the Word (*Logos*), which is itself an hypostasis. . . ." And in another passage he writes: "Though in many things the angels are superior to us, yet in a certain way they are none the less inferior. . . . They are so, for example, in respect of existence according to the image of the Creator; for in this sense we are created more perfectly conformable to the image of God. . . ."

and in principle all other forms and all states of existence belong to him because his "inward reality" is identified with that of the whole universe.

From this it will be understood why the term "Universal Man" has two meanings which coincide or are distinct according to the point of view adopted. On the one hand this name is applied to all men who have realized Union or "the Supreme Identity", to men such as the great spiritual mediators and especially the prophets and the "poles"[4] among the saints. On the other hand this name designates the permanent and actual synthesis of all states of Being, a synthesis which is at the same time both an immediate aspect of the Principle and the totality of all relative and particular states of existence. This is the Unique Prototype (*al-Unmūdhaj al-farīd*) or "clear Prototype" spoken of in the Qur'ān and already mentioned above. It should also be recalled that from the Divine "point of view" creation is integrated in this prototype in which are reflected all the Divine Qualities or "relationships" (*nisab*) without their being either confused or separated; it is only from the point of view of the creature that the universe appears as multiple. Now the great mediators, whose spirit is identified with the Divine Spirit, are by this fact related to this synthesis of the universe, the great Prototype, which is the unique and direct "object" of the Divine Act.[5]

It is to Universal Man, who is at the same time the Spirit, the totality of the universe, and the perfect human symbol, that the epithets refer which are traditionally applied to the Prophet when they are taken according to their esoteric meaning. He is "the Glorified" (*Muḥammad*) because he is the synthesis of the divine radiance in the cosmos; he is the perfect "slave" (*'abd*) because wholly passive in relation to God inasmuch as he is distinct from Him in his created nature; he is a "messenger" (*rasūl*) because, being in essence the Spirit, he emanates directly from God; he is "unlettered" (*ummī*) through the fact that he receives his knowledge directly from God without the intermediary of written signs, i.e. without any creature being an inter-

[4] The Pole of a spiritual hierarchy (or the Pole of a period, who may be unknown to most spiritual men).

[5] See also my introduction to *De l'Homme Universel* by 'Abd al-Karim al-Jīlī (fasc. II of the collection "Soufisme", Algiers and Lyons, 1953). [*Universal Man*, trans. Angela Culme-Seymour (Roxburgh: Beshara Publications, 1983).]

mediary, and he is also the unique and universal "beloved" (*ḥabīb*) of God.[6]

[6] From the Christian point of view the Unique Prototype is none other than the Son. The Son is identified with the Word, uncreated in its nature, or, to use the Christian expression, eternally "engendered" by the Father being "of the same essence" (*homoousios*) as He. As we know, Islam rejects the symbolism of Divine Sonship, for the very reason that it denies all "inner" distinction in the Divine Nature, the Names and Divine Qualities being only "extrinsic" aspects of God. This theological position of Islam, which also determines Sufi language, on the one hand respects the inability of most men to conceive of such a distinction without projecting a duality into the Divine order—and this is the relatively exoteric reason for the rejection of Divine Sonship—and on the other hand also affirms the Supreme Unity of the Divine Essence. In this respect it coincides with the theology of the Eastern Church inasmuch as the Church equally affirms that the Essence (*Ousia*) is beyond Being and thus beyond every distinction, such as that of the three Hypostases.

Chapter 13

UNION IN THE DOCTRINE OF MUḤYI-D-DĪN IBN ʿARABĪ

In his *Wisdom of the Prophets* Muḥyi-d-Dīn ibn ʿArabī describes supreme Union as a mutual interpenetration of Divinity and man; God, as it were, takes on human nature; the Divine nature (*al-Lāhūt*) becomes the content of human nature (*an-Nāsūt*), the latter being considered as the recipient of the former, and, from another angle, man is absorbed and, as it were, enveloped by Divine Reality. God is mysteriously present in man and man is obliterated in God. All this must be understood only from the spiritual point of view, or in other words according to a perspective, not of pure doctrine, but related to spiritual realization. In setting side by side these two reciprocal modes of the interpenetration of God and man Ibn ʿArabī adds, in the chapter on Abraham, that "here are two aspects of one and the same state, which are neither merged together nor yet added one to the other".

In the first mode God reveals Himself as the real Self which knows through the faculties of perception of man and acts through his faculties of action. In the second and inverse mode man moves, so to speak, in the dimensions of the Divine Existence, which in relation to him is polarized so that to each human faculty or quality there corresponds a Divine aspect. This is expressed in the sacred utterance (*ḥadīth qudsī*): "He who adores Me never ceases to approach Me until I love him, and, when I love him I am the hearing by which he hears, the sight by which he sees, the hand with which he grasps and the foot with which he walks."

In so far as it is united to the Divine Spirit, man's spirit knows all things principially since henceforward nothing is outside his own essence, but this essential and global knowledge only becomes differentiated in so far as the light of intellect falls on individual things. On the other hand the individual subject of the Divine Man inevitably subsists in a certain manner: it no longer subsists in the sense that it is only in his identification with the Divine Intellect that this being, who still bears the name of man, really feels that he is "himself"; nevertheless, if the individual subject did not subsist in any sense whatsoever, there would be no "subjective" continuity linking together his human experiences.

Now every individual subject is under certain limitations inherent in the realm in which it exists. Ibn ʿArabī expresses this by saying that the Seal of Sanctity[1] (*Khātim al-Wilāyah*), who is both the prototype and the pole (*Quṭb*) of all spiritual men, is both "the knower and ignorant" and that seemingly contradictory qualities can be attributed to him: ". . . in his essential Reality (*Ḥaqīqah*) (inasmuch as his spirit is identified with the uncreated Spirit) and in his spiritual function (which arises spontaneously from this identification) he knows (in a global and undifferentiated way) all that of which he is ignorant by his bodily constitution (which is subject to the conditions of time and space). . . . He knows and at the same time does not know; he perceives and at the same time does not perceive (his principial knowledge being beyond distinctive perception); he contemplates (the Divine Realities in his spirit) and yet does not contemplate (them individually). . ." (*The Wisdom of the Prophets*, the chapter on Seth).

In the man who is spiritually perfect the relationship between the Divine Reality (*Ḥaqīqah*) and the still subsisting individuality is one of the most difficult things to grasp.[2] For the man who has arrived at this perfection the Divine Reality is indeed no longer "veiled" by anything, whereas individual consciousness is by very definition a "veil" (*ḥijāb*) and exists only inasmuch as it "refracts" the blinding light of the Divine Intellect.

Ibn ʿArabī compares the individuality of a man who has "realized God" to a screen which colors pure light by filtering it and is, in the case of such a man, more transparent than in the case of other men. In the chapter on Joseph of his *Wisdom of the Prophets* he says: "It is like light projected through shadow, for the screen is of the nature of shadow which is itself luminous by its transparence. Such also is the man who has realized God; in him the 'form of God' (i.e. the sum of

[1] Sanctity, in the sense of the Arabic word *wilāyah*, is a permanent state of knowledge of God, a state in which there are, however, different degrees.

[2] Moreover, it is for this reason that the Christian dogma of the two natures of Christ, as well as that of the Trinity which is intimately linked with it, is a "mystery", which means that it is beyond the reach of discursive reason.

the Divine Qualities)[3] is more directly manifested than it is in the case of others. . . .”

Union with God is also conceived under the aspect of “assimilations of the Divine Qualities” (*al-ittiṣāf biṣ-Ṣifāt al-ilāhiyah*), an assimilation which must be understood in a purely intellective sense as knowledge of the Divine Qualities or Presences (*Ḥāḍarāt*).[4] Again, this “assimilation of the Divine Qualities” has its symbolical reflection in the soul in the form of the spiritual virtues and its model is nothing other than “Universal Man”.

And now, to return to what was said at the beginning of this chapter as to the mutual penetration of the Divinity and perfect man. Ibn ʿArabī compares this penetration to the assimilation of food, which is a symbol of assimilation by knowledge. God “feeds” on man and for his part man “feeds” on God; he “eats” God. The ritual expression of the former of these modes is to be found in sacred hospitality, the traditional model of which is the hospitality of Abraham to the Angels of the Lord and to the poor. He who gives food to the “divine guest” gives himself as food to God. And this recalls the Hindu proverb that “man becomes food for the Divinity he adores”. The second mode corresponds to the invocation of God, for, by the enunciation of the Name of God, man assimilates to himself the Divine Presence.[5] The Christian Eucharist clearly symbolizes the same aspect of Union.

[3] The totality of the Divine Qualities constitutes what Sufism calls the “Divine Form” (*aṣ-Ṣūrat al-ilāhiyah*) by allusion to the saying of the Prophet: “God created Adam in His form.” Thus the word “form” (*Ṣūrah*) has here the meaning “qualitative synthesis” and not that of a delimitation. It is analogous to the Peripatetic idea of *eidos* or *forma* as opposed to *hyle* or *materia*.

[4] By “Divine Presences” are to be understood the degrees of the Divine Reality considered as states of contemplation. Five chief Presences are spoken of and these are: *an-Nāsūt*, related to the human bodily form, *al-Malakūt*, related to the world of subtle Lights, *al-Jabarūt*, analogous to existence beyond form, *al-Lāhūt*, the Presence of the Divine Nature revealing Itself in the Perfect Qualities, and *al-Hāhūt*, the Pure Essence. There are also other ways in which the “Presences” are distinguished.

[5] “Man shall not live by bread alone, but by every word that proceedeth out of the mouth of God” (St. Matthew’s Gospel, 4:4, and Deuteronomy, 8:3).

PART THREE

SPIRITUAL REALIZATION

Chapter 14

THREE ASPECTS OF THE WAY: DOCTRINE, VIRTUE, AND SPIRITUAL ALCHEMY

"Operative" Sufism, like every way of contemplation, and quite apart from its differentiation according to various "paths", includes three elements or constituent aspects. These are: doctrine, spiritual virtue, and an art of concentration which we shall call, using the expression of certain Sufis, "spiritual alchemy".[1]

The assimilation of doctrinal truths is indispensable, but of itself it does not bring about a transformation of the soul, except in very exceptional cases in which the soul is so well disposed for contemplation that even a glimpse of the doctrine is enough to plunge it into contemplation, even as a supersaturated solution may, even under the very slightest shock, suddenly be transmuted into crystals. In itself doctrinal intelligence is purely static; it may deliver the soul from certain tensions but cannot truly transform it without the concurrence of will, which represents the dynamic element of the way. It may even quite easily come about that intuition of metaphysical truths, first awakened by study of doctrine, gets worn away little by little in one who supposes that he possesses these truths and adheres to them only in his mind, as if will had no part to play in relation to them.

The will must become "poor" in relation to God, or in other words it must conform to spiritual virtue, which represents a sort of latent concentration of the soul and so forms a solid and natural basis for directly operative concentration having as its aim to pierce the veil of a consciousness continually absorbed by the current of forms. "Spiritual virtue (*al-iḥsān*)", said the Prophet, "is that thou shouldest adore God as if thou didst see Him, and, if thou dost not see Him, He none the less sees thee."

[1] The most usual Arabic term is *al-kimiyā as-saʿādah*, the literal meaning of which is "the alchemy of bliss". This term al-Ghazzālī uses in a more general and external sense than that which is intended here.

According to the particular nature of the "path"—and "there are as many paths as there are human souls"[2]—doctrinal understanding plays a part of greater or lesser importance. A very extensive learning in matters of doctrine is not called for; understanding must develop in depth and not in superficial extent. For one who aspires to gnosis what matters most is that he should be as conscious of the deep meaning of the rites he carries out as his intuition will permit of. In this domain a purely quantitative effort and a blind effort of will cannot attain to anything, for knowledge can be attained only by that which is of the same nature as knowledge.

To this it must be added that in spiritual practices there are always elements which, so to speak, offer no foothold for theoretical intelligence. The fact that the Divine Truth infinitely surpasses its prefigurations in the mind must of necessity by marked in the economy of the spiritual life. In this connection one can even notice a certain inversion of relationship, for it is those supports which are the least discursive and the most "obscure" from the point of view of reasoning which, generally speaking, are the vehicles for the most powerful influences of grace. At the borderland of pure contemplation symbols become more and more synthetic and likewise more and more simple in their form.

The Divine Reality is at the same time Knowledge and Being. He who seeks to approach that Reality must overcome not only ignorance and lack of awareness but also the grip which purely theoretical learning and other "unreal" things of the same kind exert on him. It is for this reason that many Sufis, including the most outstanding representatives of gnosis such as Muḥyi-d-Dīn ibn ʿArabī and ʿOmar al-Khayyām affirmed the primacy of virtue and concentration over doctrinal learning.

It is the truly intellectual who have been the first to recognize the relative nature of all theoretical expressions. The intellectual aspect of the Way includes both a study of the doctrine and getting beyond this by intuition. If error is always strictly excluded, the mind—which is both a vehicle for truth and at the same time, in a certain sense, limits it—must itself also be eliminated in unitive contemplation.

[2] This Arab saying should not be taken quite literally. It only means that the diversity in individual natures leads to a diversity of spiritual methods. The various types of mind can always be classified in a certain number of categories.

Virtue is a qualitative form of the will; to speak of a form is to speak of an intelligible essence. Spiritual virtue is centered on its own essence and this is a Divine Quality. This means that spiritual virtue implies a kind of knowledge. According to Aḥmad ibn al-ʿArīf it is to be distinguished from virtue in the ordinary sense by the fact of being pure from any individual interest. If it implies a renunciation, that renunciation is not made in order to obtain some later recompense, for it bears its fruit within itself, fruit of knowledge and beauty. Spiritual virtue is neither a mere negation of the natural instincts—asceticism is only the very smallest step to such virtue—nor yet, of course, is it merely a psychic sublimation. It takes birth from a presentiment of the Divine Reality which underlies all objects of desire—noble passion is nearer to virtue than is anguish—and this presentiment is in itself a sort of "natural grace" which is a compensation for the sacrificial aspect of virtue.

Later, the progressive unfolding and flowering of this presentiment is answered by an ever more direct irradiation of the Divine Quality of which virtue is the trace in man, and, inversely, virtue grows in proportion as its divine model is revealed. It is the kernel of intuition which gives to spiritual virtue its inimitable quality and makes it as it were a divine mercy. Through it the Intellect radiates, not in a "sapiential", but in an "existential" mode, in beauty of soul or in the miraculous effects which the affinity between a virtue and its divine model may unloose in the cosmic surroundings.

In its intellective wholeness knowledge is in essence something supra-individual because it is universal. The virtues retrace in the individuality and in an existential mode the stages or the modes of knowledge and they are consequently reflections of knowledge, not cerebral and fleeting reflections, but reflections firmly fixed in the will; in other words they are acquisitions of being and not improvisations of thought. For this very reason virtues are indispensable supports of knowledge and this is why Sufis identify them with spiritual degrees.

This brings us to the theory of the spiritual "state" (*al-ḥāl*) and the spiritual "station" (*al-maqām*) which must be briefly mentioned. In this sense of the term a "state" is a passing immersion of the soul in the Divine Light. According to their intensity and duration "states" are spoken of as "glimmers" (*lawāʾiḥ*), "flashes" (*lawāmiʿ*), "irradiation" (*tajallī*), etc. A "station" is a "state" that has become permanent. The correspondence between the various "stations" and spiritual virtues is inevitably very complex; the ethical trace of a spiritual degree is the more subtle as the degree is more lofty and the incommensurability between the Reality contemplated and the human receptacle more profound. The various psychological definitions of the spiritual stations have above all a speculative or suggestive value.

The spiritual virtues, like the Divine Qualities which they reflect in the human order, can be considered separately and distinctly with greater or lesser degrees of differentiation, or they can be summed up in a few fundamental types. Also, virtues which are seemingly in opposition may be based on one and the same attitude of the soul. Thus patience (*aṣ-ṣabr*) and zeal (*al-ghayrah*), the second of which shows itself in holy wrath, both imply an unshakeable inner axis and this immutability shows itself passively in patience and actively in holy wrath.

In a sense all the virtues are contained in spiritual poverty (*al-faqr*) and the term, *al-faqr*, is commonly used to designate spirituality as a whole. This poverty is nothing other than a *vacare Deo*, emptiness for God; it begins with the rejection of passions and its crown is the effacement of the "I" before the Divinity. The nature of this virtue clearly shows the inverse analogy which links the human symbol with its divine archetype: what is emptiness on the side of the creature is plenitude on the side of the Creator.

Another virtue which can be taken as a synthesis of all that is implied in the attitude of being "poor" (*faqīr*) is sincerity (*al-ikhlāṣ*) or veracity (*aṣ-ṣidq*). This is the absence of egocentric preoccupations in both intentions and thoughts; ultimately it is the effacing of the mind before the Divine Truth. Thus, like "poverty", it is an emptiness of the individual and correlatively a plenitude of a higher order, though with this difference that, whereas "poverty", like humility, belongs only to the servant, veracity belongs first of all to the Lord, though it could none the less be said that the "poverty" or "humility" of God is the simplicity of His Essence.

In any case spiritual sincerity implies cessation of that split consciousness which is the ordinary state of the soul, in which man instinctively and inevitably introduces between the world (including his own actions) and God the pseudo-principle of the ego, instead of seeing the world, and his actions, with the eye of Divine Truth. He who is sincere (*aṣ-ṣiddīq*) is independent in respect of congenital or spontaneous suggestions of his "I"; he takes no delight in this "I" and leaves his left hand in ignorance of what his right hand is doing.

We have already seen that Muḥyi-d-Dīn ibn ʿArabī puts total love at the top of his "ladder" of the dwelling places of the soul. Love can therefore be considered as the synthesis of all the virtues, and indeed, if every virtue is a form of the will, then spiritual love is the will itself transfigured by the divine attraction. Love of God is imperfect and is even inconceivable apart from love of God in creation (in every aspect of His Revelation including pure intellect) and without love of (the very least) creature in God. In a sense it can be said that man must love God first in creation, in His Revealed Word and in His Truth, and then secondly in Himself, in His transcendent Ipseity, and finally in those "least of His little ones" who require our charity.

Again, from another angle, all spiritual virtues may be said to be summed up in sanctity (*al-wilāyah*) which is uninterrupted awareness of the Divine Presence.

It has been said above that doctrinal understanding can achieve nothing without virtue; the inverse of this is only true in a lesser degree, always provided that the soul clings to truth in some revealed form. Virtue is the indirect basis for spiritual concentration, for a vicious soul is not able long to concentrate on truth, and, inversely, spiritual concentration contributes to the developing of virtues. In a certain sense contemplative virtue cannot become perfected without the help of an inner "alchemy" which watches over the transmutation of the natural powers of the soul,[3] but it is through its object, the revealed symbol, that concentration opens the way to the Grace which transforms the soul.

The term "alchemy" is very suitable as applied to the art of concentration considered in itself because, from the point of view of this art, the soul is like "a matter" which is to be transformed even as in alchemy lead is to be transmuted into gold. In other words the chaotic

[3] In several respects the Sufi theory of the spiritual virtues differs from that found in the monastic teaching of the Eastern Orthodox Church. Thus, Sufis do not generally look on chastity as a basic virtue but rather as the natural result of the presence of several other virtues.

and opaque soul must become "formed" and crystalline. Here, form does not mean a fixation within certain limits but on the contrary a quasi-geometric co-ordination, and hence even a virtuality of deliverance from the limiting conditions of the arbitrary psychic tyranny, just as gold or crystal manifests on the level of solid substances the nature of light, the second both by its geometrical form—the propagation of light being rectilinear—and by its transparence.

According to the same symbolism—the nearest to alchemy properly so called—the soul, fixed in a state of sterile hardness, must be "liquefied" and then again "congealed" in order to be rid of its impurities. This "congelation" will in its turn be followed by a "fusion" and this again by the final "crystallization". In order to bring about these changes the natural forces of the soul are actualized and coordinated. They may be compared to the forces of nature—heat, cold, moistness, and dryness. There is in the soul an expansive force which normally shows itself as confident joy (*basṭ*) and as love and so as "heat", and there is a contractive force—a "coldness"—which shows itself as fear, its spiritual form being the extreme contraction (*qabḍ*) of the soul, in face of death and eternity, into the single point of the present.

As for moistness and dryness these correspond respectively to the "liquefying" passivity of the soul and the "fixing" activity of the spirit. These four forces can also be connected with two complementary principles which are analogous to the "Sulfur" and "Mercury" of the alchemist. In the Sufic method these two principles are to be identified respectively with the spiritual act—the active affirmation of a symbol—and the plasticity of the psyche. Thanks to the intervention of Grace the voluntary affirmation of the symbol becomes the permanent activity of the Spirit (*ar-Rūḥ*) while the plasticity or receptivity of the soul takes on a cosmic amplitude.[4]

The fiery quality and the "fixative" quality are connected with the active pole which corresponds to Sulfur, while the contracting quality and the "moist" dissolving quality are connected with the passive pole, which is the Mercury of alchemy. Thus it is easy to see how the different "natural" qualities of the soul are combined in different states. Sterile hardening of the soul results from an alliance between the fixing quality (dryness) of the mind and the contracting quality in

[4] According to Muḥyī-d-Din ibn ʿArabī the universal meaning of Sulfur is the Divine Act (*al-Amr*) and that of Mercury, Nature as a whole (*Tabīʿat al-kull*).

the psyche. Dissipation, on the other hand, comes from a link between the expansive force of desire and the dissolving power of the passive psyche. Moreover these two states of disequilibrium may be piled one upon the other, as is often the case. Equilibrium of the soul consists in a steady alternation of expansion and contraction, comparable to breathing, and in a marriage of the "fixative" activity of the spirit with the "liquid" receptivity of the soul.

In order that it may be possible for this synthesis to take place the powers of the soul must not let themselves be determined in any way by impulsions coming from outside; they must instead respond to the spiritual activity centered on the heart.[5]

The art of concentration has been indicated here in alchemical terms because these bring out the correspondence between the powers of the soul and the natural forces—the physical forces one might say—of the human organism. The process of harnessing these powers brings this aspect of *Taṣawwuf* near to the methods of *Raja Yoga*. Clearly the technique in question can be described by means of different symbolisms. Sufi writers usually treat of this question implicitly by indicating the use of the symbols which are the object of concentration; indeed the "alchemical" work, in the sense in which it is envisaged here, cannot be separated from the nature of the symbols used as "means of Grace" and these symbols are the intermediary through which the "alchemical" aspect of spiritual work is linked with its intellectual aspect. The pre-eminent spiritual means of *Taṣawwuf* is the verbal symbol repeated either inwardly or aloud with or without a synchronizing of the breath; hence the various phases of the inner alchemy—the successive "liquefactions" and "crystallizations"—appear as permutations (*taṣrīf*) of the symbol in the soul in conformity with the different Divine Realities (*ḥaqāʾiq*) it expresses.

During invocation of a Name of God, the three constituent aspects of the Way—doctrinal truth, virtue in the will, and spiritual alchemy—are summed up in a single inner act; virtue is the human reflection of the divine aspect symbolized by the sacred Name while the spiritual alchemy will result, in its most intimate working, from the theurgic power of that same Name, which is mysteriously identical with God.

[5] This corresponds to what in alchemy is called the "hermetic sealing" of the vessel.

Doctrine is addressed to what is "naturally" metaphysical in man; spiritual virtue and concentration have for their aim the dissolution of the knot of egocentricity which prevents the heart from directly contemplating Divine Realities. Since the individual affirmation is made of volition, virtue seizes the ego through the medium of its volitive manifestations. It may come about that a turning round of the will suddenly unveils the center of consciousness so that a renunciation, a sacrifice, or a "conversion" (*at-tawbah*) may in certain cases bring with it, suddenly, the vision of the "eye of the heart" (*ʿayn al-qalb*). As for spiritual alchemy, this transmutes the psychophysical structure of man both by acting on the organic seats of consciousness and by becoming the vehicle for the radiation of Grace, which is mysteriously present in the divine symbols.

To end this chapter we shall quote this saying of the master al-ʿArabī al-Ḥasanī ad-Darqāwī which sums up more than one aspect of the Way: "The perception (the spiritual glimpse: *al-maʿnā*) is most subtle; it can only be retained with the help of the sensory (*al-ḥiss*) and can only be made to endure by spiritual conversation (*al-mudhakkarah*), invocation (or 'recollection' of God: *adh-dhikr*), and the breaking of natural habits (both passive and instinctive)."

Chapter 15

THE INTELLECTUAL FACULTIES

The hierarchic "placing" of the faculties of the soul is one aspect of the reintegration of the soul into the Spirit. The state of a soul which has been spiritually regenerated has already been compared to a crystal which, though solid, is akin to light both in its transparence and in its rectilinear form. The various intellectual faculties are like the facets of this crystal, each one reflecting in its own way the unique and limitless Intellect.

The faculty which is specific to man is thought (*al-fikr*). Now the nature of thought, like the nature of man, is two-faced. By its power of synthesis it manifests the central position of man in the world and so also his direct analogy with the Spirit. But its formal structure, on the other hand, is only one existential "style" among many others; that is to say it is a specific mode of consciousness which could be called "animal" were it not distinguished, for better and for worse, by its connection with man's unique—and intrinsically "supernatural"—function from those faculties of knowledge that are proper to animal species. In fact thought never plays an entirely "natural" part in the sense of being a passive equilibrium in harmony with the cosmic surroundings. To the degree that it turns away from the Intellect, which transcends the terrestrial plane, it can only have a destructive character, like that of a corrosive acid, which destroys the organic unity of beings and of things.

We have only to look at the modern world with its artificial character devoid of beauty and its inhumanly abstract and quantitative structure in order to know the character of thought when given over to its own resources. Man, the "thinking animal", must necessarily be either the divine crown of nature or its adversary,[1] and this is so because in the mind "to be" becomes dissociated from "to know" and

[1] In animals there does not exist, as in man, a refraction of the intellect which is at the same time subjective and active, a refraction which would stand between the intellectual essence immanent in the form of the species and the individual psychic organism. For this reason animals are more passive than man in relation to the cosmic surroundings. At the same time they more directly express their intellectual essence. The beauty of a sacred art—an art divinely inspired—heightens that of virgin nature,

in the process of man's degeneration this leads to all other ruptures and separations.

This double property of thought corresponds to the principle which Sufis symbolize by the *barzakh*, the "isthmus" between two oceans. The *barzakh* is both a barrier and a point of junction between two degrees of reality. As an intermediate agent it reverses the pencil of rays of the light it transmits in the same manner as does a lens. In the structure of thought this inversion appears as abstraction. Thought is only capable of synthesis by stripping itself of the immediate aspect of things; the more nearly it approaches the universal, the more it is reduced as it were to a point. Thought thus imitates on the level of form—and hence imperfectly—the essential "stripping bare" (*tajrīd*) of the Intellect.

The Intellect does not have as its immediate object the empirical existence of things but their permanent essences which are relatively "non-existing" since on the sensory plane they are not manifested.[2] Now this purely intellectual knowledge implies direct identification with its object and that is the decisive criterion which distinguishes intellectual "vision" from rational working of the mind. This "vision" does not, however, exclude sensory knowledge; rather it includes it since it is its essence, although a particular state of consciousness may exclude one in favor of the other.

Here it must be made quite plain that the term "intellect" (*al-ʿaql*) is in practice applied at more than one level: it may designate the universal principle of all intelligence, a principle which transcends the limiting conditions of the mind; but the direct reflection of Universal Intellect in thought may also be called "intellect" and in this case it corresponds to what the ancients called reason.

while the creations of a civilization that is profane and practically atheistical, such as modern civilization, are always hostile to natural harmony.

[2] When certain modern thinkers would see in the act of knowing a sort of annihilation—relative and subjective—of the object of knowledge considered as pure existence they merely reproduce the unreal and implicitly absurd character of thought which has turned aside from intellectual principles and ended by emptying itself of any qualitative content. The crude and undifferentiated "existence" which these philosophers oppose to the intellectual act of the subject is nothing but the shadow cast by this absence of intuition in their own thought: it is pure unintelligibility. What is real "in itself" is essence; if perception does not simultaneously grasp all aspects of a sensory object that is because both the level of manifestation and the knowledge are alike relative.

The mode of working of the mind which is complementary to reason is imagination (*al-khayāl*). In relation to the intellectual pole of the mind imagination may be considered as its plastic material; for this reason it corresponds by analogy to the *materia prima* on which the plastic continuity of the "cosmic dream" depends just as, subjectively, it depends on imagination.

If the imagination can be a cause of illusion by binding the intelligence to the level of sensory forms it none the less also has a spiritually positive aspect in so far as it fixes intellectual intuitions or inspirations in the form of symbols. For imagination to be able to assume this function it must have acquired in full measure its plastic capacity; the misdeeds of imagination come not so much from its development as from its being enslaved by passion and feeling. Imagination is one of the mirrors of Intellect; its perfection lies in its remaining virginal and of wide compass.

Some Sufi writers, including ʿAbd al-Karīm al-Jīlī, have said that the dark pole of the mind is *al-wahm*, a term which means conjecture and also opinion, suggestion, and suspicion and so mental illusion. This is the reverse of the speculative freedom of the mind. The power of illusion of the mind is, as it were, fascinated by an abyss; it is attracted by every unexhausted negative possibility. When this power dominates the imagination, imagination becomes the greatest obstacle to spirituality. In this context may be quoted the saying of the Prophet that "the worst thing your soul suggests to you is suspicion".

As for memory, this has a double aspect; as the faculty of retaining impressions it is passive and "earthly" and it is called *al-ḥafẓ* in this relationship; in so far as it is the act of recollection (*adh-dhikr*) it is directly connected with the intellect, for this act refers implicitly to the timeless presence of the essences, although they cannot appear as such in the mind. The recapitulation of perceptions in recollection may be inadequate and in a certain sense even must be so since the mind is subject to the attrition of time, but, if recollection were not implicitly adequate, it would be only pure illusion—something which does not exist. If recollection can evoke the past in the present it is because the present contains in virtuality the whole extension of time; all existential "flavors" are contained in the "flavorlessness" of the present moment. This is what is realized by spiritual recollection (*dhikr*): instead of going back "horizontally" into the past it addresses itself "vertically" to the essences which regulate both past and future.

The Spirit (*ar-Rūḥ*) is both Knowledge and Being. In man these two aspects are in a way polarized as the reason and the heart. The heart marks what we are in the light of eternity, while the reason marks what we "think". Seen from one angle the heart (*al-qalb*) also represents the presence of the Spirit in both aspects, for it is both the organ of intuition (*al-kashf*) and also the point of identification (*wajd*) with Being (*al-Wujūd*). According to a divine saying (*ḥadīth qudsī*) revealed through the mouth of the Prophet, God said: "The heavens and the earth cannot contain Me, but the heart of my believing servant does contain Me." The most intimate center of the heart is called the mystery (*as-sirr*), and this is the inapprehensible point in which the creature meets God. Ordinarily the spiritual reality of the heart is veiled by the egocentric consciousness; this assimilates the heart to its own center of gravity which will be either mind or feeling according to the tendencies of the particular being.

The heart is to the other faculties what the sun is to the planets: it is from the sun that these receive both their light and their impulsion. This analogy, which is even more clear in the heliocentric perspective than in the geocentric system of the ancients where the sun occupies the middle heaven between two triads of planets,[3] was developed by ʿAbd al-Karīm al-Jīlī in his book *Al-Insān al-Kāmil* ("Universal Man"). According to this symbolical order, Saturn, the most distant of the planets that are visible to the naked eye, corresponds to intellect-reason (*al-ʿaql*). Just as the heaven of Saturn includes all the other planetary heavens, intellect-reason embraces all things; moreover the "abstract", cold, and "saturnian" character of reason is opposite to the solar and central nature of the heart, which marks intellect in its "total" and "existential" aspect. Mercury symbolizes thought (*al-fikr*), Venus imagination (*al-khayāl*), Mars the conjectural faculty (*al-wahm*), Jupiter spiritual aspiration (*al-himmah*), and the moon the vital spirit (*ar-rūḥ*). Anyone with some knowledge of astrological "aspects" can readily deduce from this outline both the beneficent and the harmful "conjunctions" of the different faculties represented by the planets.

From another point of view the heart is compared to the moon which reflects the light of the divine sun. In this case the phases of the moon correspond to the different states of receptivity of the heart

[3] Cf. the author's *Une Clef spirituelle de l'Astrologie musulmane d'après Mohyi-d-din Ibn Arabi* (Paris: Les Éditions Traditionnelles, 1950). [*Mystical Astrology According to Ibn ʿArabī*, trans. Bulent Rauf (Louisville: Fons Vitae, 2001.)]

or, parallel with this, to different "revelations" (*tajalliyāt*) of Divine Being.[4]

Al-himmah signifies the force of decision, the desire to rise above oneself or spiritual aspiration. Thus it is a quality of the will and not an intellectual faculty; none the less it should be noted that by anticipation spiritual will is intellectual. From the point of view of realization it is the most important and the noblest faculty of man. Man is only truly man through his will to be delivered, by his ascending tendency, pictured in his vertical posture which distinguishes him from animals. *Al-himmah* is also the faith that moves mountains.

The vital spirit, called *ar-rūḥ* by analogy with the transcendent Spirit, is what Hindus call *prāṇa* and alchemists *spiritus*: it is a subtle modality intermediate between the immortal soul and the body. It is to the Divine Spirit as the circumference of a circle is to its center. This vital spirit is relatively undifferentiated; it includes not only the spatially delimited body but also the sensory faculties with their spheres of experience. Ordinarily man is not aware of it, but in certain states of realization this spirit becomes the vehicle for a diffused spiritual light which may even radiate externally.

The sensory faculties may themselves become supports for the Spirit or mirrors which refract its light. Also every sensory faculty—whether it be hearing, seeing, smelling, taste, or touch—implies a unique essence which distinguishes it in quality from the other faculties, and this essence has its prototype in Pure Being. For the spiritual man who realizes Being in relation to one of these prototypes the respective faculty becomes the direct expression of Universal Intellect so that he either "hears" the eternal essences of things or "sees" them or "tastes" them.[5] From another angle, intuition appears of itself in one case or another as a "hearing" (*samāʿ*), as a "vision" (*ruʾyah*), or as a "taste" (*dhawq*) which is intellective in its nature.

It was said above that the two faces of the Spirit, the ontological and the intellectual, are respectively reflected in the heart and the reason. At a more external level the existential aspect of the Spirit is reflected in speech, the complement of reason; indeed the Universal Spirit is at the same time Intellect (*ʿAql*) and Word (*Kalīmah*), the

[4] See the study of astrology according to Ibn ʿArabī mentioned in the previous note.

[5] See also *De l'Homme Universel*, my translation into French of extracts from *Al-Insān al-Kāmil* by ʿAbd al-Karīm al Jīlī (Paris: Derain, 1953). [*Universal Man*, trans. Angela Culme-Seymour (Roxburgh: Beshara Publications, 1983).]

direct "enunciation" of Being. Both these aspects are to be found in the Greek word *Logos* which means principle and also idea and speech; in the same way man is defined either as a "thinking animal" or as an "animal endowed with speech" (*ḥayawān nāṭiq*).

From the principial point of view the idea is dependent on the Word, inasmuch as it is an intellectual reflection of Reality, but in man the idea precedes speech. In the rite of invocation (*dhikr*) the principial relationship is symbolically re-established since the revealed speech—the sacred formula or the Divine Name which is invoked—affirms the ontological continuity of the Spirit whereas thought is—practically speaking—cut off from its transcendent source through being the seat of individual consciousness. In this way the faculty of speech, which is a faculty of action, becomes the vehicle for knowledge of Being.

Chapter 16

RITES

A rite is an action the very form of which is the result of a Divine Revelation. Thus the perpetuation of a rite is itself a mode of Revelation, and Revelation is present in the rite in both its aspects—the intellectual and the ontological. To carry out a rite is not only to enact a symbol but also to participate, even if only virtually, in a certain mode of being, a mode which has an extra-human and universal extension. The meaning of the rite coincides with the ontological essence of its form.

For people of modern education and outlook a rite is usually no more than an aid in promoting an ethical attitude; it seems to them that it is from this attitude alone and from nothing else that the rite derives its efficacy—if indeed such people recognize in rites any efficacy at all. What they fail to see is the implicitly universal nature of the qualitative form of rites. Certainly a rite bears fruit only if it is carried out with an intention (*niyah*) that conforms to its meaning, for according to a saying of the Prophet, "the value of actions is only through their intentions", though this clearly does not mean that the intention is independent of the form of the action.[1] It is precisely because the inward attitude is wedded to the formal quality of the rite—a quality which manifests a reality both ontological and intellectual—that the act transcends the domain of the individual soul.

The quintessence of Muslim rites, which could be called their "sacramental" element, is the Divine Speech for which they provide a vehicle. This speech is moreover contained in the Qur'ān, the recitation of the text of which by itself constitutes a rite. In certain cases this recitation is concentrated on a single phrase repeated a definite number of times with the aim of actualizing its deep truth and its particular grace. This practice is the more common in Islam because the Qur'ān is composed in great part of concise formulas with a rhythmical sonority such as lend themselves to litanies and incanta-

[1] Rites of consecration are an exception because their bearing is purely objective. It is enough that one should be qualified to carry them out and that one should observe the prescribed and indispensable rules.

tions. For exotericism ejaculatory practices can have only a secondary importance; outside esotericism they are never used methodically, but within it they in fact constitute a basic method.

All repetitive recitation of sacred formulas or sacred speech, whether it be aloud or inward, is designated by the generic term *dhikr*. As has already been noted this term bears at the same time the meanings "mention", "recollection", "evocation", and "memory". Sufism makes of invocation, which is *dhikr* in the strict and narrow sense of the term, the central instrument of its method. In this it is in agreement with most traditions of the present cycle of humanity.[2] To understand the scope of this method we must recall that, according to the revealed expression, the world was created by the Speech (*al-Amr, al-Kalīmah*) of God, and this indicates a real analogy between the Universal Spirit (*ar-Rūḥ*) and speech. In invocation the ontological character of the ritual act is very directly expressed: here the simple enunciation of the Divine Name, analogous to the primordial and limitless "enunciation" of Being, is the symbol of a state or an undifferentiated knowledge superior to mere rational "knowing".

The Divine Name, revealed by God Himself, implies a Divine Presence which becomes operative to the extent that the Name takes possession of the mind of him who invokes It. Man cannot concentrate directly on the Infinite, but, by concentrating on the symbol of the Infinite, attains to the Infinite Itself. When the individual subject is identified with the Name to the point where every mental projection has been absorbed by the form of the Name, the Divine Essence of the Name manifests spontaneously, for this sacred form leads to nothing outside itself; it has no positive relationship except with its Essence and finally its limits are dissolved in that Essence. Thus union with the Divine Name becomes Union (*al-waṣl*) with God Himself.

The meaning "recollection" implied in the word *dhikr* indirectly shows up man's ordinary state of forgetfulness and unconsciousness (*ghaflah*). Man has forgotten his own pretemporal state in God and this fundamental forgetfulness carries in its train other forms of forget-

[2] This cycle begins approximately with what is called the "historical" period. The analogy between the Muslim *dhikr* and the Hindu *japa-yoga* and also with the methods of incantation of Hesychast Christianity and of certain schools of Buddhism is very remarkable. It would, however, be false to attribute a non-Islamic origin to the Muslim *dhikr*, first because this hypothesis is quite unnecessary, secondly because it is contradicted by the facts, and thirdly because fundamental spiritual realities cannot fail to manifest themselves at the core of every traditional civilization.

fulness and of unconsciousness. According to a saying of the Prophet, "this world is accursed and all it contains is accursed save only the invocation (or: the memory) of God (*dhikru-'Llāh*)". The Qur'ān says: "Assuredly prayer prevents passionate transgressions and grave sins but the invocation of God (*dhikru-'Llāh*) is greater" (29:45). According to some this means that the mentioning, or the remembering, of God constitutes the quintessence of prayer; according to others it indicates the excellence of invocation as compared with prayer.

Other Scriptural foundations of the invocation of the Name—or the Names—of God are to be found in the following passages of the Qur'ān: "Remember Me and I will remember you . . ." or: "Mention Me and I will mention you . . ." (2:152); "Invoke your Lord with humility and in secret. . . . And invoke Him with fear and desire; Verily the Mercy of God is nigh to those who practice the 'virtues' (*al-muḥsinīn*), those who practice *al-iḥsān*, the deepening by 'poverty' (*al-faqr*) or by 'sincerity' (*al-ikhlāṣ*) of 'faith' (*al-imān*) and 'submission' to God (*al-islām*)" (7:55, 56). The mention in this passage of "humility" (*taḍarru'*), of "secrecy" (*khufyah*), of "fear" (*khawf*) and of "desire" (*ṭama'*) is of the very greatest technical importance. "To God belong the Fairest Names: invoke Him by them" (7:180); "O ye who believe! when ye meet a (hostile) band be firm and remember God often in order that ye may succeed" (8:45). The esoteric meaning of this "band" is "the soul which incites to evil" (*an-nafs al-ammārah*) and with this goes a transposition of the literal meaning, which concerns the "lesser holy war" (*al-jihād al-aṣghar*), to the plane of the "greater holy war" (*al jihād al-akbar*). "Those who believe and whose hearts rest in security in the recollection (or: the invocation) of God; Verily is it not through the recollection of God that their hearts find rest in security?" (13:28).

By implication the state of the soul of the profane man is here compared to a disturbance or agitation through its being dispersed in multiplicity, which is at the very antipodes of the Divine Unity. "Say: Call on *Allāh* (the synthesis of all the Divine Names which is also transcendent as compared with their differentiation) or call on *ar-Raḥmān* (the Bliss-with-Mercy or the Beauty-with-Goodness intrinsic in God); in whatever manner ye invoke Him, His are the most beautiful Names" (17:110); "In the Messenger of God ye have a beautiful example of him whose hope is in God and the Last Day and who invokes God much" (33:21); "O ye who believe! invoke God with a frequent invocation (*dhikran kathīrā*)" (33:41); "And call on God with a pure heart (or: with a pure religion) (*mukhliṣīna lahu-d-dīn*) . . ." (40:14); "Your Lord has said: Call Me and I will answer you . . ." (40:60); "Is it not time for those who believe to humble their hearts at the remembrance of God? . . ." (57:16); "Call on (or: Remember) the Name of thy Lord and consecrate thyself to Him with (perfect) consecration" (73:8); "Happy is he who purifies himself and invokes the Name of his Lord and prayeth" (87:14, 15).

To these passages from the Qur'ān must be added some of the sayings of the Prophet: "It is in pronouncing Thy Name that I must die and live." Here the connection between the Name, "death", and "life" includes a most important initiatic meaning. "'There is a means for polishing everything which removes rust; what polishes the heart is the invocation of God, and no action puts so far off the chastisement of God as this invocation.'[3] The companions said: 'Is not fighting against infidels like unto it?' He replied: 'No: not even if you fight on till your sword is broken'"; "Never do men gather together to invoke (or: to remember) God without their being surrounded by angels, without the Divine Favor covering them, without Peace (*as-sakīnah*) descending on them, and without God remembering them with those who surround Him"; "The Prophet said: 'The solitaries shall be the first.' They asked: 'Who are the solitaries (*al-mufridūn*)?' And he replied: 'Those who invoke much'"; "A Bedouin came to the Prophet and asked: 'Who is the best among men.' The Prophet answered: 'Blessed is that person whose life is long and his actions good.' The Bedouin said: 'O Prophet! What is the best and the best rewarded of actions?' He replied: 'The best of actions is this: to separate yourself from the world and to die while your tongue is moist with repeating the Name of God'";[4] "A man said: 'O Prophet of God, truly the laws

[3] According to the *Viṣṇu-Dharma-Uttara* "water suffices to put out fire and the rising of the sun (to drive away) shadows; in the age of Kali repetition of the Name of *Hari* (*Viṣṇu*) suffices to destroy all errors. The Name of *Hari*, precisely the Name, the Name which is my life; there is not, no, there surely is no other way." In the *Mānava Dharma-Śāstra* it is said: "Beyond doubt a brahmin (priest) will succeed by nothing but *japa* (invocation). Whether he carries out other rites or not he is a perfect brahmin." Likewise also the *Mahābhārata* teaches that "of all functions (*dharmas*) *japa* (invocation) is for me the highest function" and that "of all sacrifices I am the sacrifice of *japa*".

[4] Kabīr said: "Just as a fish loves water and the miser loves silver and a mother loves her child so also Bhagat loves the Name. The eyes stream through looking at the path and the heart has become a pustule from ceaselessly invoking the Name."

of Islam are many. Tell me a thing by which I can obtain the rewards.' The Prophet answered: 'Let your tongue be ever moist with mentioning God.'"

The universal character of invocation is indirectly expressed by the simplicity of its form and by its power of assimilating to itself all those acts of life whose direct and elemental nature has an affinity with the "existential" aspect of the rite. Thus the *dhikr* easily imposes its sway on breathing, the double rhythm of which sums up not only every manifestation of life but also, symbolically, the whole of existence.

Just as the rhythm inherent in the sacred words imposes itself on the movement of breathing, so the rhythm of breathing in its turn can impose itself on all the movements of the body. Herein lies the principle of the sacred dance practiced in Sufi communities.[5] This practice is the more remarkable since the Muslim religion as such is rather hostile both to dancing and to music, for the identification through the medium of a cosmic rhythm with a spiritual or divine reality has no place in a religious perspective which maintains a strict and exclusive distinction between Creator and creature. Also there are practical reasons for banishing dancing from religious worship, for the psychic results accompanying the sacred dance might lead to deviation. None the less the dance offers too direct and too primordial a spiritual support for it not to be found in regular or occasional use in the esoterism of the monotheistic religions.[6]

[5] According to a *ḥadīth*, "He who does not vibrate at remembrance of the Friend has no friend". This saying is one of the scriptural foundations of the dance of the dervishes.

[6] A Psalm in the Bible says: "Let them praise His Name in the dance: let them sing praises unto him with the timbrel and the harp." It is known that the sacred dance exists in Jewish esoterism, finding its model in the dancing of King David before the Ark of the Covenant. The apocryphal Gospel of the Childhood speaks of the Virgin as a child dancing on the altar steps, and certain folk customs allow us to conclude that these models were imitated in mediaeval Christianity. St Theresa of Avila and her nuns danced to the sound of tambourines. Mā Ananda Moyi has said: "During the *samkīrtana* (the 'spiritual concert' which is the Hindu equivalent of the Muslim *samā*ʿ, or rather, of *ḥadra* or ʿ*imāra*) do not pay attention to the dance or the musical accompaniment but concentrate on His Name.... When you pronounce the Name of God your spirit begins to appreciate the *samkīrtana* and its music predisposes you to

It is related that the first Sufis founded their dancing *dhikr* on the dances of the Arab warriors. Later, Sufi orders in the East, such as the Naqshabandis, adapted certain techniques of *hatha-yoga* and so differentiated their form of dance. Jalāl ad-Dīn Rūmī, who founded the Mevlevī order, drew the inspiration for the collective *dhikr* of his community from the popular dances and music of Asia Minor.[7] If the dances and music of the dervishes are mentioned here it is because these are among the best known of the manifestations of Sufism; they belong, however, to a collective and so to a rather peripheral aspect of *taṣawwuf* and many masters have pronounced against their too general use. In any case, exercises of this kind ought never to preponderate over the practice of solitary *dhikr*.

Preferably invocation is practiced during a retreat (*khalwah*), but it can equally be combined with all sorts of external activities. It requires the authorization (*idhn*) of a spiritual master. Without this authorization the dervish would not enjoy the spiritual help brought to him through the initiatic chain (*silsilah*) and moreover his purely individual initiative would run the risk of finding itself in flagrant contradiction to the essentially non-individual character of the symbol, and from this might arise incalculable psychic reactions.[8]

the contemplation of divine things. Just as you should make *pūjās* and pray, you should also take part in *samkīrtanas*."

[7] An aesthetic feeling can be a support for intuition for the same reason as a doctrinal idea and to the extent to which the beauty of a form reveals an intellectual essence. But the particular efficacy of such a means as music lies in the fact that it speaks first of all to feeling, which it clarifies and sublimates. Perfect harmony of the active intelligence (the reason) and the passive intelligence (feeling or sensibility), prefigures the spiritual state—*al-ḥāl*.

[8] "When man has made himself familiar with *dhikr*", says al-Ghazzālī, "he separates himself (inwardly) from all else. Now at death he is separated from all that is not God. . . . What remains is only invocation. If this invocation is familiar to him, he finds his pleasure in it and rejoices that the obstacles which turned him aside from it have been put away, so that he finds himself as if alone with his Beloved. . . ." In another text al-Ghazzālī expresses himself thus: "You must be alone in a retreat . . . and, being seated, concentrate your thought on God without other inner occupation. This you will accomplish, first pronouncing the Name of God with your tongue, ceaselessly repeating: *Allāh, Allāh,* without letting the attention go. The result will be a state in which you will feel without effort on your part this Name in the spontaneous movement of your tongue" (from his *Iḥyā᾽ ʿUlūm ad-Dīn*). Methods of incantation are diverse, as are spiritual possibilities. At this point we must once again insist on the danger of giving oneself up to such practices outside their traditional framework and their normal conditions.

Chapter 17

MEDITATION

Meditation (*at-tafakkur*) is an indispensable complement of the rites because it gives value to the free initiative of thought. None the less its limitations are those of the mind itself; without the ontological element of rites it could not pass from the separateness (*al-farq*) of individual consciousness to the synthesis (*al-jamʿ*) of consciousness beyond form. In Islam it is founded on the verses of the Qurʾān addressed to "those endowed with understanding" and recommending for meditation the "signs" (the symbols) of nature; it is also founded on these two sayings of the Prophet: "One hour (one moment) of meditation is worth more than the good works accomplished by the two species of beings endowed with weight (men and jinns, *jinnah*)" and: "Meditate not on the Essence but on the Qualities of God and on His Grace".

Normally meditation proceeds with a circular motion. It starts from an essential idea, developing its diverse applications in order in the end to reintegrate them in the initial truth which thus acquires for the intelligence that has reflected on it a more immediate and a richer actuality. This is the opposite of philosophical research, which envisages truth as something not already in essence present in the mind of him who seeks to know it. The true movement of thought is the circular movement followed by meditation, and all philosophy which disregards this is mistaken in its procedure. The truth which philosophy seems to find by dint of arguments is already implicit in its point of departure unless at the end of a long maze of thought the philosopher merely "rediscovers" the mental refraction of some old prejudice born of passion or individual or collective pre-occupation.

Individualist thought always includes a blind spot because it is unaware of its own intellectual essence. As for meditation, although it fails to grasp the Essence directly, it does at least presuppose it. Meditation is a "wise ignorance", whereas the philosophical ratiocination which arises from mental individualism is an "ignorant learnedness".

When philosophy scrutinizes the nature of knowledge it is inevitably in a dilemma. When it separates the subject from the objective domain and attributes to it a wholly relative reality in the sense of individual "subjectivity", it forgets that its own judgments depend on the reality of the subject and its capability of affirming the truth; when, on the other hand, it declares that all perceptions or intellections are merely "subjective", and therefore relative and uncertain, it forgets that by this very assertion it is in fact laying claim to objectivity. For thought there is no way out of this dilemma. The mind, which is only a particle of the universe, only one of the modalities of existence, can neither embrace the universe nor yet define its own position in relation to the whole. If it none the less attempts this task it is because there is in it a spark of the Intellect, and the Intellect does embrace and really penetrate all things.

The second *ḥadīth* on meditation quoted above means that the Essence can never become the object of thought, for thought is by nature distinctive while the Essence is one. On the other hand meditation does in a certain fashion conceive the Divine Qualities though without directly "tasting their flavor"—for that is something which belongs to the domain of pure intuition.

The proper domain of meditation is discrimination of the real from the unreal and the chief object of such discrimination is the "I". Meditative discrimination does not directly reach the root of subjective individuation but does grasp its extrinsic aspects which represent so many elements of disproportion between a quasi-absolute affirmation, implied in the ego, and the ephemeral and fragmentary character of individual human nature. It must be clearly understood that it is not this individual nature as such which constitutes the egocentric illusion; the "veil" (*al-ḥijāb*) which has to be rent is only the attributing to this individual nature of an autonomous and "aprioric" character which belongs only to the Essence.[1]

[1] The fact that the perfect sage is conscious of his individual nature does not imply that he is duped by it and so does not prevent him from going beyond illusion.

Chapter 18

CONTEMPLATION, ACCORDING TO MUḤYI-D-DĪN IBN ʿARABĪ

According to Ibn ʿArabī the "spiritual state" (*al-ḥāl*), the sudden illumination of the heart, is brought about by the reciprocal action of the divine "irradiation" (*at-tajallī*),[1] and the "predisposition" of the heart (*al-istiʿdād*). According to the point of view adopted, one or the other of these two poles will appear as the determining factor and the other as the determined.

In face of the Divine, Formless, and Omnipresent Reality, which no quality could define, the particular character of a spiritual state could only be attributed to the predisposition of the heart, that is, to the basic and intimate receptivity of the soul, according to the well-known parable of al-Junayd: "the color of water is the color of the vessel containing it."

On the other hand the predisposition of the heart is only pure potentiality. It cannot be known apart from the divine irradiation, for potentiality can only be fathomed in so far as its contents are actualized. Now it is the irradiation which actualizes the predisposition of the heart; it is the irradiation which gives to the spiritual state its intelligible quality. It is, says Ibn ʿArabī, "evident by itself" for it affirms itself immediately and positively in the spiritual state as a divine "aspect" or "Name", whereas the predisposition as such remains—as our author puts it in his *Wisdom of the Prophets* (the chapter on Seth)—"the most hidden thing there is".

According to this latter aspect of things there is thus nothing in the heart's receptivity which is not response to the divine irradiation or revelation, the lightning flashes of which it intermittently receives. These flashes vary according to the different "aspects" or "Names"

[1] It has already been pointed out that *at-tajallī* means both "irradiation" and "revelation" and also "unveiling". To understand the relationship linking the ideas of "unveiling" and "irradiation" we must recall the image of the sun which radiates immediately the clouds are dispersed. The same ambivalence of aspects is to be found in this verse of the Qurʾān: "By the night when it covers and by the day when it unveils (or: when it irradiates) (*tajallā*). . ." (*Sūrat* of the Night, 92:1-2).

of God and the process is never exhausted either on the side of the divine irradiation, which is essentially inexhaustible, or on the side of the primordial plasticity of the heart.

Ibn ʿArabī himself takes his stand alternately at one or other of these points of view. On the one hand he affirms that the divine "content" of illumination cannot be grasped and that only the receptive "form" of the heart—a "form" which unfolds itself starting from the basic predisposition of the being in question—imparts its quality or "color" to the irradiation. On the other hand he says that the "form" the heart takes on in contemplation of God is wholly wedded to the modes of the irradiation. What the recipient can impose on the divine irradiation is in fact only a limitation, and this limitation is nil compared with its qualitative content. What is manifested in it, and, in a sense, because of it, is nothing other than a Divine Quality (*Ṣifah*) or Reality (*Ḥaqīqah*) included in the one and Infinite Essence.

The two points of view contradict one another in appearance because the one relates to the manifestation of God in Universal Qualities, a manifestation which is in a sense "objective", whereas the other is turned towards the "subjective" reality of the Essence. Ibn ʿArabī writes as follows on this subject in the chapter on Jethro of the book already quoted:

> . . . the heart of the gnostic (*al-ʿarif*)[2] has an amplitude such that Abū Yazīd al-Bisṭāmī said of it that if the Divine Throne with all It surrounds were to be found a hundred million times in a corner of the gnostic's heart he would not feel it. And Junayd says in the same sense that, if the ephemeral and the eternal are joined, there remains no trace of the former; how then should the heart which contains the eternal feel the existence of the ephemeral?—But the divine irradiation may vary in its form; so the heart must enlarge or contract at the will of this irradiation, for in no respect could it withdraw from the modalities of the irradiation. . . . This is the opposite of what the men of our Way envisage when they say that God reveals Himself according to the measure of the predisposition of the worshipper, for it is not thus that we understand it.

[2] The term "gnostic" is used according to its etymological sense, in which it was also taken by Christian Fathers such as St. Clement of Alexandria, and without regard to its application to certain sects.

It is the worshipper who manifests himself to God according to the "form" in which God reveals (*tajallā*) Himself to him.

The master goes on to explain that the predisposition is based on the being's essence (*al-ʿayn ath-thābitah*) and is thus the expression of what this being is in himself as a permanent possibility contained in God. In this sense it is in the principial state of non-manifestation (*al-ghayb*) that the "heart", the essential and imperishable "kernel" of the being, receives its "predisposition". God "communicates" it to him in the mystery of the pure Aseity (*al-huwiyah*) and then reveals Himself to him in an "objective" manner by imprinting on him the "forms" of His "Names" or "aspects", "in such wise that the one sees the other and the heart in its turn manifests itself in the aspect of that which is revealed to it. . ." (chapter on Jethro).

Thus, the spiritual polarity of "irradiation" and "predisposition" finally appears as the purely metaphysical polarity of Being (*al-Wujūd*) and the "immutable essences" (*al-aʿyān ath-thābitah*) included in the unmanifest "abyss" of Essence. Being "overflows" (*afāda*) into the immutable essences inasmuch as these posit implicitly the constitutive distinctions or limitations of the world, but of themselves these distinctions are nothing and add nothing to the light of Being, just as the immutable essences are not really distinct from the One Essence (*adh-Dhāt*). From another angle it may be said that it is by refracting Being that the relative possibilities contained in the archetypes are realized in their various modes, and it is in relation to these same relative possibilities that Divine Being is in Its turn polarized as so many personal aspects. It must be evident that this global picture of things is quite unconnected with any psychological, or even with any alchemical or mystical explanation. It has no other purpose than that of providing an intellectual key which can help man to pass beyond the antithesis of subject and object.

Considered in this way the "predisposition of the heart", or its aptness to receive a particular divine revelation, is not merely psychological. None the less it has a certain psychological aspect which is like the shadow of what it is in its essence. One can retrospectively grasp certain modes of the predisposition: one can get a glimpse of it by the aid of symbols; but these are only imperfect perceptions.[3]

[3] These perceptions are not unrelated to what Buddhism describes as recollection of existences preceding the individual's earthly life.

As a whole it must always elude the grasp of one's consciousness. The "predisposition" can only directly be known through its intellectual integration into the archetype,[4] an integration which is outside any created order: ". . . For it is clearly beyond the faculties of the creature as such . . . to know with Divine Knowledge which embraces the archetypes (*al-aʿyān ath-thābitah*) in their unmanifest state, these archetypes being only pure relationships (within) the Essence and without form. . . . (Thus direct knowledge of the basic predisposition of a being is only possible through its participation in the Divine Knowledge), a participation which represents predestined divine aid to this being . . . by virtue of a certain content of his own immutable essence" (from the chapter on Seth).

This knowledge of one's own archetype is indeed knowledge of Self (*Ātman*), to use an expression borrowed from Hindu doctrine, or the Aseity or Ipseity (*al-huwiyah*), to use a Sufi term. Such knowledge may be called divinely "subjective" since it presumes a definitive or incidental identification of the spirit with the Divine "Subject" and in it God does not appear as the "object" of contemplation or knowledge. It is, on the contrary, the relative subject, the ego, which is—in its principial possibility—the "object" in relation to the Universal and Absolute Subject, the only Subject there is, in so far as such distinctions are still applicable on the "divine level".[5] Thus the "point of view" implied in knowledge of the Self is in a way the inverse of that implied in "objective" contemplation of God in His Names and Qualities, though this latter "vision" cannot be attributed to the relative subject as such, for in reality it is not we who contemplate God but God Himself who contemplates Himself in His Qualities for the manifestation of which we are supports.

In His Infinite and Impersonal Essence (*Dhāt*) God does not become the "object" of any knowledge. He always remains the implicit witness (*Shāhid*) of every cognitive act, that by which or in which every being knows itself. "Vision comprehendeth Him not, but He comprehendeth (all) vision" (Qurʾān, 6:103). The Divine Witness

[4] Principially speaking potentiality is reducible to possibility, which is itself permanent, and not potential, in the Divine Intellect.

[5] They are applicable in their principial reality, but not as regards the psychological and material limitations to which they are subject on the level of the creature. In the principial order "subject" and "object" are the two poles of all knowledge—the "knower" (*al-ʿāqil*) and the "known" (*al-maʿqūl*).

cannot be "grasped", because it is He who "grasps" all things.[6] In the same way spiritual identification with the Divine Subject proceeds from that Subject. This Ibn ʿArabī expresses by saying it is realized "by virtue of a certain content of the immutable essence of that being, a content he himself will recognize as soon as God makes him to see it". This is as much as to say that knowledge of oneself flows from the "Self". Spiritual identification with the Divine Subject has, however, intellectual prefigurings, which anticipate its actual realization, and realization itself can have degrees of actualization in man although in itself essential identification allows of no gradations; at every one of these degrees the relative subject is "objectivized" more or less perfectly.[7]

"The Essence (*adh-Dhāt*)", says Ibn ʿArabī, "reveals Itself only in the 'form' of the predisposition of the being who receives this 'revelation'; it is never otherwise. Thenceforward he who receives the 'revelation' of the Essence (*Tajallī dhātī*) sees in the Divine Mirror only his own 'form'. He will not see God—it is impossible that he should see Him—though knowing that he sees his own 'form' only by virtue of this Divine Mirror. This is wholly analogous to what takes place in the case of the material mirror. When you contemplate forms in it you do not see the mirror, though you know it is only thanks to the mirror that you see these forms—or your own form. God has manifested this phenomenon as a symbol especially appropriate to the revelation of His Essence so that he to whom God reveals Himself should know that he sees Him not. . . . So force yourself to see the body of the mirror while looking at the form reflected in it: never will you see both at the same time. So true is this that some, having observed this law of the reflection in mirrors (whether material or spiritual), have held that the reflected form is interposed between the sight of him who contemplates and the mirror itself, and this is the loftiest thing they have grasped in the domain of intellectual knowledge" (from the chapter on Seth).

[6] In Vedantic doctrine too the Absolute Subject is called the "Witness" (*Sākṣin*).

[7] The methodic objectivizing of one's relative subject—the empirical ego—and its identifying in essence with the "point of view" of the Divine Subject is indicated in this definition of spiritual virtue (*al-iḥsān*) in the *ḥadith Jibrīl* already quoted: "Adore God as if thou didst see Him, and, if thou dost not see Him, none the less He sees thee."

In reality it is as we have said above—that is, that the reflected "form" does not essentially hide the mirror, since the mirror manifests the form and we know implicitly that we see it only by virtue of the mirror. The spiritual point of view inherent in this symbolism is analogous to that of the Vedānta. This impossibility of grasping the mirror "objectively" at the same time as we contemplate our image in it expresses the ungraspable character of *Ātman*, the Absolute "Subject", of which all things, including the individual subject, are only illusory "objectivations". Like the expression "Divine Subject", the symbol of the mirror evokes a polarity whereas the Essence is beyond all dualism such as that of "subject" and "object": this, however, is something no symbol could express.

Ibn ʿArabī goes on: "If you savor this (that the being who contemplates never sees the very Essence but sees his own 'form' in the mirror of Essence) then you savor the utmost limit to which the creature can attain. Do not aspire beyond this, nor tire your soul to pass beyond this degree (in an 'objective' mode), for beyond there is, in principle and definitively, only pure non-existence. . . ." But this does not mean the Essence cannot be known: "Some among us are ignorant of the direct knowledge of God and in this connection quote the saying of the Caliph Abū Bakr: 'To grasp that one is powerless to know knowledge is a knowledge';[8] but there is among us one who really knows and who does not express himself thus, because his knowledge implies no powerlessness to know; it implies the inexpressible" (from the chapter on Seth).

The master sums up all that has been explained above in these words, also from the chapter on Seth: "Thus God is the mirror in which you see yourself, as you are. His mirror in which He contemplates His Names. Now his Names are not other than Himself, so that the analogy of relations is an inversion."

[8] In its deepest meaning this saying is akin to the Vedantic discrimination between the pure "subject", *Ātman*, and its illusory "objectivation" as the individual subject or *jīva*.

GLOSSARY AND INDEX

N.B.—Dates quoted below are given as dates of Christian era.

al-ʿabd: the servant, the slave; in religious language designates the worshipper, and, more generally, the creature as dependent on his Lord (*rabb*). 10.

ʿAbd al-Karīm al-Jīlī, ibn Ibrāhīm, c. 1365-c. 1417; a Sufi. Among his writings is the well-known *Al-Insān al-Kāmil* ("Universal Man"). 6, 19, 25, 60, 66n, 85, 86.

ʿAbd al-Qādir Jīlānī, 1077-1166, one of the greatest saints in Islam and the founder of the Qādiriyah order. 4n, 112.

ʿAbd ar-Razzāq al-Qashānī: a Sufi of the thirteenth century, a commentator on Ibn ʿArabī. 56, 57.

ʿAbd as-Salām ibn Mashīsh: a famous Sufi; lived in the twelfth century in the Jabala mountains of Morocco; master of Abu-l-Ḥasan ash-Shādhilī. 11.

Abu-l-Ḥasan ash-Shādhilī, 1196-1252, a great Sufi master, founder of the Shādhilīyah order. 21.

al-Aḥadiyah: the Transcendent Unity; in Sufism means the Supreme Unity which is not the object of any distinctive knowledge, and which is therefore not accessible to the creature as such. Only God Himself knows himself in His Unity. As a spiritual state this Unity implies the extinction of every trace of the created. 18, 44, 45, 115.

Aḥmad ibn al-ʿArīf: an Andalusian Sufi of the twelfth century, author of the *Maḥāsin al-Majālis*. 23, 30n, 77, 110.

ʿālam al-ajsām: "the world of bodies". 56. See also *ʿālam al-arwāḥ*.

ʿālam al-arwāḥ: "the world of (pure) spirits" distinguished from *ʿālam al-mithāl*, "the world of analogies", which is formal manifestation as a whole including both the psychic and the physical worlds. 55. See also *ʿālam al-jabarūt*.

ʿālam al-jabarūt: "the world of Omnipotence", sometimes identified with *ʿālam al-arwāḥ*: "the world of (pure) spirits"; manifestation beyond form. 55, 71. See also *Hāhūt*.

ʿālam al-mithāl, or *ʿālam al-amthāl*: "the world of analogies", the world of forms, both psychic and corporeal; corresponds to *ʿālam al-khayāl*, "the world of imagination". 56. See also above, *ʿālam al-arwāḥ*.

Ali, ibn Abi Ṭālib: the cousin and son-in-law of the Prophet and the fourth Caliph of Islam. 36, 60.

al-Amr: the order, the commandment; in theology: the divine Command symbolized by the creative word *kun*, "be": "His command (*amruhu*), when He wills a thing, is that He says to it: 'be' and 'it is'" (Qur'ān, 36:82). The Command corresponds to the Word, and indeed in Aramaic the word *amr* has this meaning. By implication the following two passages from the Qur'ān affirm the identity of the Command and the Divine Word: "In the sight of God Jesus is what Adam is. God created him from dust; then He said to him: Be! (*Kun*) and he was" (3:59). "The Messiah, Jesus, son of Mary, is the messenger of God and His word (*kalimatuhu*) which He projected on to Mary, and His spirit" (4:171). *Al-Amr* often has the meaning "reality", "act", "something real". The Qur'ān says: "Unto God shall return the realities (*al-umūr*)", and this clearly means that the uncreated essences of things will return to God. Thenceforward these essences are identified with the Divine Command and are contained in it. The Divine Command corresponds to the Pure Act and, as such, is opposed to the pure passivity of Nature (*aṭ-Ṭabīʿah*). 15, 51, 58, 59, 61, 80n, 90.

anfās: plural of *nafas*. 57.

al-ʿāqil: the knower, the intelligent. In metaphysic the triad *al-ʿāqil* (the knower), *al-maʿqūl* (the known), and *al-ʿaql* (the intellect, knowledge) play an important part. 100n.

al-ʿAql: the intellect. 84, 86.

al-ʿAql al-awwal: the first Intellect, analogue of the Supreme Pen (*al-Qalam*), and of *ar-Rūḥ*. Corresponds to the *Nous* of Plotinus. 59, 111.

al-ʿArabī, al-Hasanī ad-Darqāwī: a famous reviver of Sufism in the Maghreb; founded the Shādhilite order of the Darqāwā; died in Morocco in 1823. 82.

al-ʿārif: the knower, the gnostic. 98. See also *maʿrifah*.

āsmāʾ dhātiyah: Names of the Essence; these are the Divine Names where there is no analogy with the creature.

asmāʾ Ṣifātiyah: qualitative Names; Names designating Divine Qualities.

al-ʿayn: the essence, the first determination, the eye, the spring. 99.

al-ʿayn ath-thābitah, or sometimes simply *al-ʿayn*: the immutable essence, the archetype or the principial possibility of a being or a thing (plural: *al-aʿyān*). 99.

ʿayn al-qalb: the eye of the heart, the organ of intellectual intuition. 82.

baqāʾ: subsistence, duration; in Sufism designates the spiritual state of subsistence beyond all form, that is, the state of reintegration in the Spirit, or even in Pure being; also means the Divine Eternity. Its opposite is *fanāʾ*, q.v. 3, 40, 106.

al-barakah: the blessing, the spiritual influence. *Shaykh al-barakah* is a phrase also used of a master who bears the spiritual influence of the Prophet or who has realized that spiritual presence which is only a virtuality in the case of most initiates. 7.

al-Bāri: the Producer. 50n.

al-barzakh: the isthmus; symbol of an intermediate state or of a mediating principle. 40, 84, 107.

al-basmalah: the Islamic formula of consecration, *bismillāhi-r-rahmāni-r-rahim* ("In the Name of God, the Compassionate, the Merciful"). 36, 37.

al-basṭ: expansion (of the soul through hope or spiritual joy); opposite of *al-qabḍ*, q.v. 80, 112.

bāṭin: inner, hidden; the opposite of *ẓāhir*, q.v. The "inner learning" (*al-ʿilm al-bāṭin*), which means esoteric or Sufic learning, is distinguished from the "outer learning" (*al-ʿilm aẓ-ẓāhir*) of the Doctors of the Law. *Al-Bāṭin*, "the Inner", is one of the Names of God in the Qurʾān. 3, 63, 115.

al-bayʿah: the pact; in the spiritual order means the rite of initiation; in the temporal order, the investiture of a sovereign. 7.

al-Bīrūnī, Abū Raihān: a learned Persian of the tenth century; wrote a famous book on the Hindu civilization. See *Alberuni's India*, edited by E. C. Sachau, Trubner's Oriental Series. 3n.

buṭūn: inwardness. 57.

ad-daqāiq: plural of *daqīqah*, finesse, subtlety. In Sufism designates the aspects of the subtle world, the psychic world, as opposed to *Ḥaqāiq* which designate the Realities of the world beyond form. 25, 26.

Darqāwiyah or *Derqawiyah*: a branch of the Shādhilīyah order in the Maghreb. 7.

adh-Dhāt: the Essence, the Quiddity. This expression is the feminine of *dhu* meaning "possessor of". The *dhāt* of a being is the subject to which all its qualities (*ṣifāt*) relate; these qualities differ as between themselves, but not in their being connected with the same subject. 45, 45n, 50, 99, 101.

adh-dhawq: literally, a "taste"; in Sufism, it relates to an intuition of the Intellect through which divine realities are perceived. 87.

dhikr: literally, "recollection" or "remembrance"; it also refers to the rite of invocation for Sufis. 82, 85, 88, 90, 90n, 91, 93-94, 94n, 108, 110.

al-fanāʾ: extinction, evanescence; in Sufism designates extinction of individual limitation in the state of Union with God. The opposite is *al-baqāʾ*, "subsistence", q.v. Cf. this verse of the Qurʾān: "Everything on it (the earth) is transitory (*fānī*); there remains only the Countenance of thy Lord, the essence of Majesty and of Bounty" (55:26-27). 3, 40.

faqīr: "poor"; the attitude of spiritual emptiness, egolessness, and humility. The term is used, by extension, to refer to the Sufi spiritual seeker who is sincerely "poor", "humble", and unambitious in spirit. 78.

al-faqr: indigence, spiritual poverty. Cf. this passage from the Qurʾān: "Oh ye men! Ye are the poor (*fuqarāʾ*) in relation to God, and it is He Who is the Independent, the Glorious" (35:15). 29, 78, 91.

al-farq: separation; separative consciousness, the opposite of *al-jamʿ*, q.v. 95.

al-fayḍ: the overflowing, outpouring, flux, effusion, emanation: *al-fayḍ al-aqdas*: "the most holy outpouring", i.e. principial manifestation. 51.

Fuṣūṣ al-Ḥikam: lit. the "Bezels of the Wisdoms". The title of a famous work by Muḥyī-d-dīn ibn ʿArabī, usually translated as "The Wisdom of the Prophets". 14n, 24, 35n, 51, 53n, 56, 56n, 111.

Futūḥāt al-Makkiyah: "The Meccan Revelations", the richest of the works of Muḥyī-d-dīn ibn ʿArabī. 50n, 58, 111.

al-ghaflah: negligence, heedlessness, unconsciousness. 90.

al-ghayb: the hidden, the mystery, the unmanifest. 99.

al-ghayrah: zeal, jealousy. It is said that God is "jealous" in the sense that He does not tolerate any other divinity being "associated" with Him. 78.

al-Ghazzālī, Abū Ḥamīd Muḥammad: 1058-1111, a great Sufi theologian and a reviver of the religious sciences of Islam. 4n, 75n, 94n.

al-Ḥabāʾ: lit. "the fine dust suspended in the air"; *Materia Prima*, the passive universal Substance. 60, 61, 107, 114.

al-Ḥāḍarāt (plural of *Ḥaḍrah*): the (divine) Presences, or the modes of Divine Presence in contemplation. 47n, 71.

ḥadīth: saying of the Prophet transmitted outside the Qurʾān through a chain of known intermediaries. There are two kinds of *aḥādīth*: *ḥadīth qudsī* (sacred sentence), a direct revelation, in which God speaks in the first person by the mouth of the Prophet, and *ḥadīth nabawī* (prophetic sentence), an indirect revelation in which the Prophet speaks as himself. 31, 31n, 44, 50, 69, 86, 93, 96, 101n, 108.

al-ḥaḍrah: the (divine) Presence; also designates collective invocation accompanied by dancing. 93, 107. See also *al-ʿimārah.*

al-ḥafẓ: memory, in the sense of faculty of retaining an impression. 85.

al-Hāhūt: The Essential Nature of God; word derived from the Divine Name *Huwa*, "He", and formed by analogy with the following terms, here given in descending hierarchical order:

al-Lāhūt: the Divine (creative) Nature.

al-Jabarūt: the Divine Power or Immensity, the world beyond form.

al-Malakūt: the Kingdom of the angels, the spiritual world.

an-Nāsūt: human nature, and in particular man's bodily form. 71n.

al-ḥāl (plural *aḥwāl*): state, spiritual state. Sometimes *ḥāl* (state) is opposed to *maqām* (spiritual station), and in this case the former is considered as a passing thing and the latter as something stable. 77, 94n, 97.

al-Ḥaqīqah: the truth, reality; in Sufism, the Divine Truth or Reality, the essential reality of a thing. Cf. this saying of the Prophet: *likulli dhī haqqin ḥaqīqah*, "to every real thing there corresponds a Divine Reality (or, Truth)". 10, 13, 29, 70, 98, 107, 113-114.

Ḥaqīqat ḥaqāʾiq: "The Truth of truths", or, "The Reality of realities", an analogue of the *Logos*; it is looked on as an "isthmus" (*barzakh*) that cannot be grasped, intermediate between the Divine Being and the cosmos. 60.

al-Ḥaqq: Truth or Reality; in Sufism designates the Divinity as distinguished from the creature (*al-khalq*) V. sup. *al-Ḥaqīqah*. 13.

haykal: temple, bodily form. 13n.

ḥayawān nāṭiq: animal endowed with speech: classical definition of man as compared with the other animal species. 88.

al-haybah: reverential fear, terror in face of the Divine Majesty. 62.

al-Hayūlā: arabicized form of Greek *Hyle*; the *Materia Prima*: analogue of *al-Ḥabā*, especially in its secondary and cosmic aspect. 60n, 61.

ḥijāb: veil, curtain. The Prophet said that God hides Himself by seventy thousand curtains of light and darkness. In Sufism, a person "veiled" (*maḥjūb*) whose consciousness is determined by passion, whether sensual or mental, so that he does not perceive the Divine Light in the heart. According to this mode of expression, it is man and not God who is covered by a veil or curtain. 14, 70, 96.

al-himmah: the force of decision, spiritual aspiration. 86, 87.

al-ḥiss: the faculty of sensation, the domain of the senses. 82.

al-ḥukm: judgment, the faculty of judging. From same root as *ḥikmat*, wisdom. 50.

al-ḥurūf (plural of *ḥarf*): the letters of the Arabic alphabet and so the sounds they represent. 58.

al-Huwiyah: word derived from the pronoun *Huwa* (He): the Divine Aseity or Ipseity, the Supreme "Self". 27, 58, 99, 100.

Ibn ʿAṭā-illāh al-Iskandarī: ob. 1309, of Shādhilīyah order, author of well-known Sufi apothegms *al-Ḥikam*. 49.

Ibrāhīm ibn Adham: famous Sufi of eighth century, a native of Balkh. 6.

al-iḥsān: sanctifying virtue, spiritual beauty. Note the fundamental triad: *al-islām* (abandonment to the Divine Will), *al-īmān* (faith), and *al-iḥsān*, on which the Prophet commented in the famous *ḥadīth* of Jibrīl. 75, 91, 101n.

Iḥyā-ʿulūm ad-dīn: "The Vivification of the Sciences of Religion"; title of a work of al-Ghazālī. 94.

ījād: bringing to existence (*Wujūd*); lit. "existentiation". 49.

al-ikhlāṣ: sincerity, purity of intention. 29, 78, 91.

imām: model, prototype; in relation to ritual: he who presides when a number pray together; head of a religious community. 63.

al-ʿimārah: technical term for collective *dhikr* accompanied by dancing; 93, 107. See also *al-ḥaḍrah*.

al-Insān al-kāmil: "the perfect man" or "the universal man"; Sufi term for one who has realized all levels of Being; also designates the permanent prototype of man. 6, 25, 65, 86, 87n, 103, 115.

al-ishārah: allusion, symbolism. 50.

al-istiʿdād: predisposition, aptitude, preparation for receiving, virtuality. 97.

al-ittiṣāf biṣ-Ṣifāt al-ilāhiyah: "assimilation of (or: to) the Divine Qualities". 71. See also *Ṣifāt*.

al-Jabarūt: the world of the Divine Omnipotence or Immensity. 55, 71n, 103, 107. See also *ʿālam al-Jabarūt* and *Hāhūt*.

Jabrāʾīl, *Jibrīl*, *Jabrīl*, or *Jabrāʾil*: the archangel Gabriel. 61, 101n.

al-jadhb: the divine attraction, or "fascination", which enters to a greater or lesser degree into every spiritual process. It is an aspect of grace. 9, 110. See also *majdhūb*.

al-Jalāl: the Divine Rigor, awe-inspiring Majesty. 38.

Jalāl ad-dīn Rūmī: 1207-73; a famous Sufi of Konya; founded the Mevlevī order of "whirling dervishes". Composed the well-known poem, the *Mathnawī* in Persian, which contains his whole doctrine. 21, 23, 94, 110.

al-jam': synthesis, union, unitive consciousness; the opposite is *al-farq*. 95, 106.

al-Jāmī, Nūr ad-dīn 'Abd ar-Raḥmān: Persian Sufi, author of the treatise *Lawā'ih*, "Flashes". Died in 898 A.H. 53.

al-jihād al-aṣghar: the lesser holy war, i.e. the external holy war against infidels. 91.

al-jihād al-akbar: the greater holy war, i.e. the inward holy war against passions and ignorance. On returning from a campaign against the infidels the Prophet said: "We have come back from the lesser holy war to the greater holy war." 91.

al-jinnah or *al-jinn*: the genii: subtle beings belonging to the world of forms. 95.

al-Junayd, Abu-l-Qāsim, ob. 910, famous master of Sufism, named "the leader of the troop". 21, 97.

karb: tautening, distress; opposed to *tanfīs* (dilation, consolation), a word derived from *naffasa* (q.v.). Before they are "dilated" in a distinctive mode the possibilities of manifestation are in a state of "contraction" when considered from the point of view of their later development, though not in their immutable reality. 57, 57n.

al-kashf: intuition; literally: "the raising of a curtain or veil". 86.

al-kawnu insānun kabīrun wa-l-insānu kawnun ṣaghīr: "The universe (or, the cosmos) is a big man and man is a little universe (or, cosmos)." Sufi saying. 65.

khalwā: seclusion, spiritual retreat. 94.

khātim or *khatam*: seal. 70.

khātim-al-Wilāyah: "the seal of Sanctity"; *khātim an-Nubuwwah*: "The seal of Prophecy". The former expression is often related to Christ at his second coming, the latter always refers to Muḥammad. 70.

al-kimiyā as-sa'ādah: "the alchemy of bliss", the title of a book by al-Ghazālī and synonymous with *al--kīmiyā ar-rūḥāniyah* (spiritual alchemy). 75n.

kun: be! The creating fiat, or order. 15, 58, 104.

al-Lāhūt: the Divine Nature; opposed to *an-Nāsūt* (human nature). Ibn ʿArabī says the latter is like a form or container of which *al-Lāhūt* is the content, or the secret life. *Lāhūt* is derived from *ilāh*, "divinity", *nāsūt* from *insān*, "man". 69, 71n, 107. See also *Hāhūt*.

lawāʾiḥ: glimmers, intuitions. *Lawāʾiḥ* is the title of a book by al-Jāmī (q.v.). 53, 77.

lawāmiʿ: flashes, sudden intuitions. 77.

al-Lawḥ al-maḥfuz: the Guarded Tablet, symbol of universal receptive Substance or of the universal Soul. 59.

al-lubb: the kernel; figuratively, the hidden meaning, the essence of a thing, the heart. The contrary is *al-qishr*, the shell: "Grasp the kernel and cast away the shell!" 3.

al-maḥabbah: love, spiritual love. 9, 22. See also *al-maʿrifah*.

Maḥāsin al-Majālis: "Beauties of the Assemblies"; title of a work of Aḥmad ibn al-ʿArīf on the spiritual virtues. 23, 30n, 103.

majdhūb: one who undergoes the divine attraction (*al-jadhb*), the spiritual man whose mental faculties are as it were paralyzed or confused by the effect of the Divine attraction. Such is the case of the "fools in God"—not of those who pretend to be mad in order to isolate themselves from men, but those who really are incapable of outwardly expressing their spiritual state in an intelligible way. 9, 109.

al-Malakūt: the Permanent Sovereignty, the celestial and angelic kingdom. Cf. this verse from the Qurʾān: "It is He Who holds in His Hand the Sovereignty of all things" (36:83). 71n, 107. See also *Hāhūt*.

al-maʿna: the meaning, signification, spiritual perception. 82.

Manṣūr al-Hāllaj, al-Ḥusayn: 858-922, crucified by the sharīʿat authority for having said *Ana-l-Ḥaqq*: "I am the Truth." 21.

al-maʿrifah: knowledge, gnosis; *al-maʿrifah* (knowledge), *al-maḥabbah* (love), and *al-makhafah* (fear) make up the Sufi triad of motives or qualities which lead towards God. 22, 28.

Mevlevī: dervish order founded by Maulanā Jalāl ad-Dīn Rūmī. 94. 109.

Mishkāh: niche, tabernacle. Cf. the *sūrat* of the "Light": "God is the light of the heavens and of the earth. The symbol of His Light is like a tabernacle (*mishkāh*); in the tabernacle there is a lamp, the lamp is in a glass; the glass is like a brilliant star. . ." (24:35). 14.

al-mudhakkarah: spiritual talk, the action of recalling (*dhikr*) to one another divine truths. 82.

al-muḥsinīn: the virtuous; those who practice the virtues. 91.

Muḥyi-d-Dīn ibn ʿArabī (sometimes: ibn al-ʿArabī) al-Hātimi, al-Andalusī, surnamed *ash-Shaikh al-Akbar* (the greatest master): 1165-1240. Wrote numerous Sufi treatises of which the most famous is his *Fuṣūṣ al-Ḥikam* and the most rich in content his *Futūḥāt al-Makkiyah*. 10, 10n, 15, 17, 19, 21, 22n, 23-25, 33n, 35n, 50n, 51-53, 53n, 56, 56n, 57n, 58, 61, 69-71, 79, 80n, 87n, 97, 98, 101-103, 106, 110, 112, 114.

al-mumkināt (plural of *mumkin*): the possibilities. In logic a distinction is made between *mumkin* (possible), *wājib* (necessary), and *jāʾiz* (contingent); from the metaphysical point of view the possible amounts principially to the necessary, since of necessity every possibility has the reality that conforms to its nature. 51.

al-murshid: the spiritual master; literally: he who leads straight. 7.

Nafas ar-Raḥmān: "The Outbreathing of the Compassionate", also called *an-Nafas Raḥmāni*: "The Merciful Outbreathing"; Divine Mercy considered as manifesting principle and thus as the quasi-maternal power of God. 57, 61.

nafassa: to breathe, breathe out, dilate, console. 57, 58n.

an-nafs: the soul, the psyche, the subtle reality of an individual, the "I". As opposed to the spirit (*rūḥ*) or to the intellect (*ʿaql*), the *nafs* appears in a negative aspect, because it is made up of the sum of individual or egocentric tendencies. But a distinction is made between: 1. *an-nafs al-ḥaywāniyah*: the animal soul, the soul as passively obedient to natural impulsions; 2. *an-nafs al-ammārah*: "the soul which commands", the passionate, egoistic soul; 3. *an-nafs al-lawwāmah*: "the soul which blames", the soul aware of its own imperfections; 4. *an-nafs al-mutmaʾinnah*: "the soul at peace", the soul reintegrated in the Spirit and at rest in certainty. The last three of these expressions are from the Qurʾān. 14, 28, 50.

an-Nafs al-kulliyah: the Universal Soul, which includes all individual souls. This corresponds to the Guarded Tablet and is the complement of the Spirit (*ar-Rūḥ*) or First Intellect (*al-ʿAql al-awwal*) and is analogous to the Psyche of Plotinus. 59, 61.

Naqshbandiyah: Sufi order of Persian origin, founded by Naqshband (1317-89), which has spread chiefly in Islamic countries in the East. 7n.

nisab kulliyah: universal relationships, universal categories. 47.

an-Nūr: light, in particular the Divine Light, uncreated, which includes all manifestation and is identified with Existence, considered as a principle. Cf. this verse from the Qur'ān: "God is the Light of the heavens and of the earth. . ." (24:35). 47n.

Omar al-Khayyām: Persian Sufi of the eleventh and twelfth centuries famous for his poems. He reacted against religious hypocrisy by veiling his spiritual allusions in skeptical language. 76.

Omar ('Umar) ibn al-Fāriḍ: 1182-1235, famous Sufi poet who wrote on Divine Love. Lived at Cairo. 23.

al-qabḍ: contraction; spiritual state following from fear of God; opposite of *al-basṭ*. 80, 105.

al-qābil (plural: *al-qawābil*): receptacle, passive and receptive substance; derived from root QBL which means "to receive", "to be in face of". 51, 112.

Qādiriyah: Sufi order founded by 'Abd al-Qādir Jīlānī. 7n, 103.

al-qadr: power, predestination, the measure of the power inherent in a thing. 33.

al-Qalam al-a'lā: the Supreme Pen; the complement of the Guarded Tablet. 61, 104.

al-qalb: the heart, the organ of supra-rational intuition, which corresponds to the heart just as thought corresponds to the brain. The fact that people of today localize feeling and not intellectual intuition in the heart proves that for them it is feeling that occupies the center of the individuality. Note the analogy between the root of the word (QLB) and the root of *qābil* (QBL) (q.v.). 14, 86.

al-Quṭb: the pole; in Sufism: the Pole of a spiritual hierarchy. The "pole of a period" is also spoken of. This pole is often unknown to most spiritual men. 70.

ar-Raḥmah: the Divine Mercy. The same root RHM is to be found in both the Divine Names: *ar-Raḥmān* (the Compassionate, He whose Mercy envelops all things) and *ar-Raḥīm* (the Merciful, He who saves by His grace). The simplest word from this same root is *raḥim* (womb), whence the maternal aspect of these Divine Names. 36, 38, 57, 57n.

rasūl: envoy, messenger; in theology: divine messenger. It is in his function of *rasūl* that a prophet (*nabī*) promulgates a new sacred law; not every prophet is necessarily a *rasūl*, although he enjoys divine inspiration, but every *rasūl* is by implication a *nabī*. 66, 113.

Risalat al-Aḥadīyah: "The Epistle of the Unity", a treatise probably by Muḥyi-d-Dīn ibn 'Arabī. 17.

ar-Rūḥ: the spirit; in Sufism this word includes the following main meanings: 1. the Divine, and therefore uncreated Spirit (*ar-Rūḥ al-ilāhi*), also called *ar-Rūḥ al-Qudūs*, the Holy Spirit; 2. the Universal, created, Spirit (*ar-Rūḥ al-kullī*); 3. the individual Spirit, or rather the Spirit polarized in relation to an individual; 4. the vital spirit, intermediate between soul and body. Cf. this verse from the Qur᾽ān: "And they will question thee on the subject of the spirit; say to them: The spirit (comes from) the command (*amr*) of my Lord . . ." (17:85). Christ is called *Rūḥ Allāh*, "Spirit of God". 14, 34, 59, 61, 65, 80, 86, 87, 90, 104, 111, 115. See also *Amr.*

ru᾽yah: vision; in its precise meaning designates formal vision, belonging to the bodily or psychic world; by an extension of the symbolism it can designate any contemplation, even beyond the level of form. *Ru᾽yat al-qalb*: "vision of the heart", spiritual intuition. 87.

aṣ-ṣabr: patience. 78.

Sahl at-Tustari, Abū Muḥammad: 818-96, a famous theologian and Sufi of Tustar in the Ahwaz, whose "Thousand Sayings" were collected by his disciples. 19n.

as-Sakīnah: the Divine Peace which dwells in a sanctuary or in the heart. The root SKN includes the meanings of immobility (*sukūn*) and of habitation. The word is analogous to the Hebrew *Shekīna* (the Divine Glory dwelling in the ark of the Covenant). Cf. this verse from the Qur᾽ān: "It is He Who makes the *Sakīnah* descend into the hearts of the believers that they may acquire a new faith over their faith. . ." (48:4). 14n, 92.

as-samāʿ: audition, hearing; also designates sessions of spiritual music. 87, 93n.

Seyidnā ʿĪsā: "Our Lord Jesus." 6.

shahādah: testimony, and in particular the testimony that "there is no divinity but The Divinity". 43.

sharīʿah: the Sacred, Revealed Law. Every Divine Messenger (*rasūl*) brings a new *sharīʿah*, according with the cyclic and human conditions. *Sharīʿah* is opposed to *Ḥaqīqah*, i.e. the Sacred Law to the Divine Truth or Reality; the Sacred Laws are different one from another, but their Divine Reality is always the same. 35n.

ash-Shuhūd: consciousness, the quality of witnessing. 47n.

ṣifāh: singular of *ṣifāt*. 105.

aṣ-ṣifāt: qualities or attributes. 46, 71, 105, 108. See also *Dhāt.*

as-silsilah: the chain; in Sufism denotes the continuity of spiritual descent from the Prophet. 4, 94.

Sirr: secret, mystery; in Sufism designates the intimate and ineffable center of consciousness, the "point of contact" between the individual and his Divine principle. 14, 86.

aṣ-ṣūfī: Sufi, adherent to Sufism; in its strictest sense designates one who has arrived at effective knowledge of Divine Reality (*Ḥaqīqah*): hence it is said: *aṣ-ṣūfī lam yukhlaq* (the Sufi is not created). 3n, 15.

Suhrawardī of Alep: a Persian Sufi, put to death in 1191 for his over-bold doctrinal expressions. 21.

aṣ-ṣūrah: form. In relation to the "form" of God, it does not designate a delimitation but a "qualitative" synthesis. 71n.

Taʿayyun: determination, individuation; also includes the meaning "auto-determination". And it is thus it must be understood in relation to God. 49, 52.

aṭ-ṭabīʿah: nature. 58, 61, 104.

Ṭabīʿat al-kull: universal Nature. An aspect of passive and "plastic" universal Substance (*al-Ḥabā*) and is that Substance inasmuch as it generates the world; hence its material nature. Ibn ʿArabī attributes to it a reality co-extensive with the whole of universal manifestation and identifies it with the "Expiration of the Compassionate". 80n.

at-Taṣawwuf: Sufism; designates the whole of the contemplative ways founded on the sacred forms of Islam. By transposition an Arab might speak on "Christian *taṣawwuf*" or "Jewish *taṣawwuf*" to indicate the esotericism of the respective Traditions. 3, 3n., 9, 21, 81, 94.

at-tajallī: unveiling, revelation, irradiation. 50, 97, 97n.

tanzīh: remoteness, exaltation, affirmation of the Divine Transcendence; the contrary is *tashbīh*: comparison, similitude, affirmation of symbolism. The two terms are to be found together in such sayings in the Qurʾān as "Nothing is like unto Him (*tanzīh*) and it is He Who sees and hears (= *tashbīh*)." 44.

tanzīl: descent; designates revelation in the theological sense, i.e. the "descent" of the sacred "Books". 33n.

ṭarīqah: See *ṭurūq*.

at-tawḥīd: the affirmation of Unity. In common usage means the saying of the Muslim credo, the recognition of the Divine Unity; in Sufism it sums up all levels of the knowledge of Unity. 22, 43.

aṭ-ṭūl: height; figuratively: the spiritual dimension of exaltation. 39.

ṭurūq (plural of *ṭarīqah*): road or path; designates the spiritual way, either The Way *par excellence* or one or other of the many esoteric ways or methods. Cf. the Sufi saying: "The ways (*ṭurūq*) towards God are as numerous as the souls of men." 7, 7n, 14.

al-ʿudum: often vocalized as *al-ʿadam*: non-existence, absence, Non-Being, nothingness. In Sufism this expression includes on the one hand the positive sense of non-manifestation, of a principial state beyond existence or even beyond Being, and on the other hand a negative sense of privation, of relative nothingness. 49, 51, 51n, 52, 57.

al-ʿumq: depth; in a figurative sense: the cosmic abyss. 39.

al-ʿUnṣur al-aʿzam: the supreme Element, Universal Substance in its Divine and unfathomable reality. 61.

al-Unmūdhaj al-farīd: the Unique Prototype: applied both to *ar-Rūḥ* and to "Universal Man" (*al-Insān al-kāmil*). Sometimes written: *Anmūdhaj*. 63, 66.

al-ʿurḍ: breadth; figuratively: the cosmic amplitude. 39.

al-Waḥdah: the Divine Solitude; stands ontologically between the Supreme Unity (*al-Aḥadīyah*) and the Distinctive Uniqueness (*al-Wāḥidīyah*). 47n.

wāḥid: one, alone. See *Wāḥidīyah*. Grammatically *wāḥid* is the adjectival form corresponding to the nominal form *aḥad* (q.v.). 44.

al-Wāḥidīyah: the (Divine) Uniqueness; is to be distinguished from the Transcendent Unity (*al-Aḥadīyah*) which is beyond all distinctive knowledge whereas the Uniqueness appears in the differentiated just as principial distinctions appear in it. 44, 45.

al-wahm: opinion, conjecture, the conjectural faculty, suspicion, illusion. 85, 86.

al-wajd: existential intuition, identification with Being (*wujūd*), ecstasies. 86.

Wajh Allāh: the Face of God; the transcendent Essence of all things. Cf. these verses from the Qurʾān: "All that is on it (the earth) is transitory and there remains only the Countenance of thy Lord, the Essence of Majesty and of Bounty." 60.

al-wārid: inspiration, in the sense of spiritual perception. 27.

ẓāhir: external; apparent; opposite of *bāṭin* (q.v.). 3, 105.

aẓ-Ẓāhir: the External, or, the Apparent, is one of the Names of God in the Qurʾān. 32, 63.

az-zuhd: ascesis, asceticism envisaged as a privation of sensory satisfactions. 13.

For a glossary of all key foreign words used in books published by World Wisdom, including metaphysical terms in English, consult: www.DictionaryofSpiritualTerms.org.
This on-line Dictionary of Spiritual Terms provides extensive definitions, examples and related terms in other languages.

BIOGRAPHICAL NOTES

TITUS BURCKHARDT (1908-1984) was a leading member of the "traditionalist" or "perennialist" school of comparative religious thought, well-known for its espousal of the "transcendent unity of religions". He was also an expert on Islam, Islamic arts and crafts, and its spiritual dimension, Sufism. In the 1930s Burckhardt visited the Islamic Maghreb where he lived for a time in the old city of Fez. There he attended courses at the Qarawiyyīn University on the traditional Islamic sciences. During the 1950s and 1960s Burckhardt presented pioneering and authoritative selected French translations of Sufi classics such as Ibn al-ʿArabī's *Fuṣūṣ al-Ḥikām* (Bezels of Wisdom), ʿAbd al-Karīm al-Jīlī's *Al-Insān al-Kāmil* (Universal Man), and Mulay al-ʿArabī ad-Darqāwī's *Rasāʾil* (Letters). In the 1970s, Burckhardt was appointed by UNESCO as special advisor to the Moroccan government, with particular reference to the preservation of the unique architectural heritage in Fez, a city whose political, cultural, and spiritual history he had recounted in his book *Fez, City of Islam*. During this period he also published the widely acclaimed *Art of Islam: Language and Meaning*, a monograph that sets forth the intellectual and spiritual principles of Islamic sacred art. In 1999 an international colloquium (called "Hommage a Titus Burckhardt") was held in Marrakesh to commemorate the exceptional achievements of his life's work. Burckhardt's other writings include: *Moorish Culture in Spain*, *Mystical Astrology According to Ibn ʿArabī*, *Alchemy: Science of the Cosmos, Science of the Soul*, *Sacred Art in East and West*, *Chartres and the Birth of the Cathedral*, and *Siena, City of the Virgin*. Four posthumous collections of his writings have also been published: *Mirror of the Intellect*, *The Foundations of Christian Art*, *The Foundations of Oriental Art* (forthcoming) and *The Essential Titus Burckhardt*.

OTHER BOOKS BY TITUS BURCKHARDT

Alchemy, Science of the Cosmos, Science of the Soul
Art of Islam: Language and Meaning
Chartres and the Birth of the Cathedral
Famous Illuminated Manuscripts
Fez, City of Islam

Introduction to Sufi Doctrine

Moorish Culture in Spain
Mystical Astrology according to Ibn 'Arabi
Sacred Art in East and West
Siena, City of the Virgin

EDITED WRITINGS OF TITUS BURCKHARDT

The Essential Titus Burckhardt:
Reflections on Sacred Art, Faiths, and Civilizations
ed. William Stoddart
The Foundations of Christian Art:Illustrated,
ed. Michael Oren Fitzgerald
The Foundations of Oriental Art: Illustrated,
ed. Michael Oren Fitzgerald
Mirror of the Intellect: Essays on Traditional Science and Sacred Art,
ed. William Stoddart

WILLIAM C. CHITTICK is a professor in the Department of Asian and Asian-American Studies at the State University of New York, Stony Brook. He is author and translator of twenty-five books and one hundred articles on Sufism, Shīʿism, and Islamic thought in general. Among his most important publications are *The Sufi Path of Love: The Spiritual Teachings of Rumi*, *The Sufi Path of Knowledge: Ibn al-ʿArabī's Metaphysics of Imagination*, *The Self-Disclosure of God: Principles of Ibn al-ʿArabī's Cosmology*, *Sufism: A Short Introduction*, *The Heart of Islamic Philosophy: The Quest for Self-Knowledge in the Teachings of Afdal al-Dīn Kāshānī*, *Me & Rumi: The Autobiography of Shams-i Tabrizi*, *Science of the Cosmos, Science of the Soul*, and *The Sufi Doctrine of Rūmī: Illustrated.* He is co-author (with Sachiko Murata) of *The Vision of Islam* and editor of *The Inner Journey: Views from the Islamic Tradition* and *The Essential Seyyed Hossein Nasr.*

Titles in the Spiritual Classics Series by World Wisdom

The Buddha Eye: An Anthology of the Kyoto School and Its Contemporaries, edited by Frederick Franck, 2004

A Christian Women's Secret: A Modern-Day Journey to God, by Lilian Staveley, 2008

Gospel of the Redman, compiled by Ernest Thompson Seton and Julia M. Seton, 2005

Introduction to Sufi Doctrine, by Titus Burckhardt, 2008

Lamp of Non-Dual Knowledge & Cream of Liberation: Two Jewels of Indian Wisdom, by Sri Swami Karapatra and Swami Tandavaraya, translated by Swami Sri Ramanananda Saraswathi, 2003

Light on the Indian World: The Essential Writings of Charles Eastman (Ohiyesa), edited by Michael Oren Fitzgerald, 2002

Music of the Sky: An Anthology of Spiritual Poetry, edited by Patrick Laude and Barry McDonald, 2004

The Mystics of Islam, by Reynold A. Nicholson, 2002

Naturalness: A Classic of Shin Buddhism, by Kenryo Kanamatsu, 2002

The Path of Muhammad: A Book on Islamic Morals and Ethics by Imam Birgivi, interpreted by Shaykh Tosun Bayrak, 2005

Pray Without Ceasing: The Way of the Invocation in World Religions, edited by Patrick Laude, 2006

The Quiet Way: A Christian Path to Inner Peace, by Gerhard Tersteegen, translated by Emily Chisholm, 2008

Tripura Rahasya: The Secret of the Supreme Goddess, translated by Swami Sri Ramanananda Saraswathi, 2002

The Way and the Mountain: Tibet, Buddhism, and Tradition, by Marco Pallis, 2008

Titles on Islam by World Wisdom

Art of Islam: Illustrated, by Titus Burckhardt, 2009

Christianity/Islam: Perspectives on Esoteric Ecumenism, by Frithjof Schuon, 2008

Introduction to Sufi Doctrine, by Titus Burckhardt, 2008

Introduction to Traditional Islam: Illustrated, by Jean-Louis Michon, 2008

Islam, Fundamentalism, and the Betrayal of Tradition: Essays by Western Muslim Scholars, edited by Joseph E.B Lumbard, 2004

The Mystics of Islam, by Reynold A. Nicholson, 2002

The Path of Muhammad: A Book on Islamic Morals and Ethics by Imam Birgivi, interpreted by Shaykh Tosun Bayrak, 2005

Paths to the Heart: Sufism and the Christian East, edited by James S. Cutsinger, 2003

Paths to Transcendence: According to Shankara, Ibn Arabi, and Meister Eckhart, by Reza Shah-Kazemi, 2006

The Spirit of Muhammad: From Hadith, edited by Judith and Michael Oren Fitzgerald, 2009

A Spirit of Tolerance: The Inspiring Life of Tierno Bokar, by Amadou Hampaté Bâ, 2008

The Sufi Doctrine of Rumi: Illustrated Edition by William C. Chittick, 2005

Sufism: Love and Wisdom, edited by Jean-Louis Michon and Roger Gaetani, 2006

Sufism: Veil and Quintessence, by Frithjof Schuon, 2007

Understanding Islam, by Frithjof Schuon, 1998

Universal Spirit of Islam: From the Koran and Hadith, edited by Judith and Michael Oren Fitzgerald, 2006